THE HOME BUYING AND SELLING

JUGGLING ACT

TIMING THE PROCESS TO MAXIMIZE PROFITS AND MINIMIZE HASSLES

Robert Irwin

DEARBORN™
A **Kaplan Professional** Company

This publication is designed to provide accurate and authoritative information in regard to the subject matter covered. It is sold with the understanding that the publisher is not engaged in rendering legal, accounting, or other professional service. If legal advice or other expert assistance is required, the services of a competent professional person should be sought.

Acquisitions Editor: Jean Iversen
Managing Editor: Jack Kiburz
Interior Design: Lucy Jenkins
Cover Design: Jody Billert
Typesetting: Elizabeth Pitts

Printed in the United States of America

99 00 01 10 9 8 7 6 5 4 3 2 1

Library of Congress Cataloging-in-Publication Data

Irwin, Robert, 1941–
    The home buying and selling juggling act : timing the processs to
maximize profits and minimize hassles / Robert Irwin.
      p. cm.
    Includes index.
    ISBN 0-7931-3199-5 (pbk.)
    1. House buying—United States.   2. House selling—United States.
I. Title.
HD255.I777   1999
643'.12—dc21   99-17447
                                   CIP

Contents

●●

1

Buy-Sell Your Home

The vast majority of homebuyers are also homesellers. In fact, though few of us think about it, most residential real estate transactions are really a kind of musical chairs with property: I'll sell my house and buy yours. You'll sell your house and buy someone else's. The person who buys my house also sold theirs. And so on.

In other words, first-time buyers are the exception, not the rule. Most buyers are property-hoppers, moving from one home to the next.

Most of us see this process as two independent transactions: the sale of the existing house on which a commission is most often paid; and the purchase of the next house, whose price usually includes another commission.

But what if instead we used the model the airlines use? One-way fares are always higher, sometimes difficult to book, and can be associated with additional stress by having to make arrangements twice. But round-trip fares are cheaper and almost always easier to book, and with the one deal, you've taken care of all your needs and you can relax.

Why not think of moving to your next home in the same way? Instead of having two separate transactions, book a round-trip flight. As part of one deal you'll sell your existing home and find and purchase a new one.

If you go for the round-trip housing ticket, here's what you stand to accomplish:

- Save big bucks with a commission discount.
- Get better deals because you have the flexibility to transfer equity.
- Get the right agent to handle both transactions.
- Take less time to sell your old home and buy the next, because it's all part of one combined deal.
- Avoid paying extra costs for storage and living expenses if you must move out of the old house before the new one is ready.
- Tie up your next house now, before prices go higher.
- Have the time to pick and choose the right financing.

Is the Round-Trip Home Transaction for You?

Not everyone can benefit from turning two deals into one. If you plan to sell and rent instead of buying, then this book probably won't be that helpful—although it will show you some selling tricks you might not have previously considered. If you're a first-time home-buyer, a round-trip is not for you—although you'll learn some unusual ways to purchase your first home for less.

You'd be wise to consider a round-trip buy-sell deal under the following conditions:

- You want to move to a better neighborhood and must sell your existing home to do so.
- You need a bigger house to accommodate a growing family.
- You want to downsize to a less physically and financially demanding place.
- You want to take advantage of the up-to-$250,000 (per person) capital gain exclusion on sale to get some cash out but still need a place to live.
- You're moving to a new area.
- You have any other reason to sell your current home and buy another one.

How Do I Do It?

If I've convinced you to consider the sale of your current home and the purchase of your next as a single larger deal, then the next question is bound to be, "How do I do it?"

The answer is to begin with a time line. You need to know what to do today, next weekend, and in the coming weeks. You need to know what to expect, how to prepare for it, and when to be ready to act.

In the next chapter, we'll take a close look at a time line that might work very well for you.

When Do I Get Started?

Have you decided to make a change in housing? If so, then the time to begin your round-trip buy-sell deal is now. Time is money, and you can waste a lot of both by sitting around waiting for something to happen. So let's get started, right now.

The Quiz: Buy-Sell Decision

Yes   No

❏   ❏   1. Is your current home too big for your needs?

❏   ❏   2. Do you have more people in your family than your current home can comfortably accommodate?

❏   ❏   3. Is the neighborhood a problem? (Does it look bad, have gangs or crime?)

❏   ❏   4. Is your current home old and falling apart?

❏   ❏   5. Do need to move to a new area for employment reasons?

❏   ❏   6. Are you going to purchase your next home (instead of renting)?

❏   ❏   7. Will you use your equity as part of your next down payment?

❏   ❏   8. Have you begun talking to agents and looking at other homes?

❏   ❏   9. Do you anticipate moving soon?

❏   ❏   10. Can you visualize the buy-sell transaction as one big deal instead of two smaller ones?

Answers

"Yes" answers indicate you're serious about a buy-sell move; "no" answers indicate the opposite.

The Buy-Sell Juggling Act

One of the most important things to remember is that selling your old home and buying a new one is part of a single process. Get a handle on the process and you can control it—and profit from it. In this chapter, we're going to get an overview of what you should do and when.

The Mistake of Using a Linear Time Line

Most of us operate on a linear track. We put one foot before another, we put our pants on one leg at a time, we start at the beginning and move to the end.

But that's not always the best way to operate. Let's consider selling an existing home and buying a new one.

Operating on a linear time line, we'd follow these seven steps in order:

1. Fix up the old home.
2. List it with an agent.
3. Wait until it sells.
4. Look for a new home.
5. Make an offer on a new home.
6. Arrange for financing.
7. Purchase the new home.

Sound familiar? This is the way that most people go about handling the buy-sell process. A number of things are wrong with progressing in a linear fashion.

House Short

If you sell your existing home first, you'll likely need to move out before you complete the purchase of your new home. Where will you live in the interim?

Furniture in Transit

Then there's the matter of your worldly possessions. What do you do with your furniture if it's in the moving van, but your new home isn't ready yet?

Scramble to Find a New Home

If you feel you must sell your old home before buying a new one, you'll find yourself scrambling in the transaction. Today escrows move rapidly, often in 30 days or less. That may not allow you enough time to identify the location in which you want to live, much less the house you want to buy.

Double Agents

In the linear time-frame world, you'll pay two commissions whether you realize it or not. Certainly you'll pay a commission to the agent who sold your home. And built into the price of the new home you buy will be part of a commission to another agent.

Financing Penalty

Because you wait to make your purchase before securing financing, you won't take advantage of "preapproval," where a lender commits to lend you money before you buy. Preapproval can provide additional leverage in an offer, possibly getting you a lower purchase price.

House Trapped

What if your old house doesn't sell? Do you just sit there waiting and waiting indefinitely?

These are just a few problems you can face if you handle the buy-sell procedure in a linear fashion. Moving ponderously, step by step, may eventually accomplish what you want, but along the way you'll gather aggravation and lose money. A better way to look at it is as if it's a juggling act.

The Buy-Sell Juggling Act

A juggler keeps a lot of balls in the air at the same time without dropping them. In short, the juggler doesn't simply do one thing after another, but more or less does all things at once. (For those who are computer-savvy, think of the difference between linear and random access.)

You need to be a bit of a juggler when you're involved in the buy-sell process. You need to do lots of things more or less at the same time. Just putting one foot after another won't do. You've got to handle a variety of things almost simultaneously. You need to become a property juggler.

Here are some of the steps you'll need to accomplish, although not necessarily in this order:

- Make an offer on a new property.
- List your old home.
- Work with an agent on both buying and selling.
- Get preapproved financing.
- Fix up your existing home.
- Make arrangements for furniture transfer.
- Survive and prosper!

Is It Possible to Do It All at Once?

Of course not. But once you get started you can work on all of it more or less simultaneously. After all, even a juggler who keeps six balls in the air doesn't get them all up there at the same time. Successful jugglers throw each ball up one at a time, and keep them going. You're going to do the same thing. In an orderly fashion, you're going to get one thing started. And while that's "up in the air," or you're in process, you're going to get started on another. Then, while you are juggling two, you'll work on starting the third, and so on until you have all of the balls in the air at the same time.

Isn't that impossible?

Not really, particularly because none of the things you'll need to do will require constant attention. You just need to get them started and then, while you wait for them to work their way along until more attention is needed, you can work on another project. In this way, you can get all things done, more or less, simultaneously.

Where Should I Start?

The usual advice is to start at the beginning.

I suggest that instead, you start in the middle. A number of steps take more time to accomplish than others, so I suggest that you begin with those.

Day One—Start Your Loan Preapproval

You'll need this when negotiating for your next house, so begin work on it immediately. Call for an appointment and fill out an application. Often you can do this the same day you begin. Then begin looking for the documents and other verifying materials you'll need to complete before approval but that can be sent in at a later time.

Once this process is started, it needs to be monitored on a weekly basis, at least. But very little time is needed to be spent directly on it.

In Chapter 3, we'll discuss where to find a loan broker and how to get preapproval online.

Day Two—Start Looking for a New Home

This is always fun and it will serve a dual purpose. In addition to helping you find your next home, it will also bring you up to date on the market so you'll have a better sense of what to ask for your existing home.

If you don't have an agent (see below), begin by picking up the local paper and looking at the For Sale ads. Check out those you might be interested in.

Also, get a map so you can plot areas to check out. Be sure your map covers the entire area where you want to live, typically spreading out a certain number of miles (or minutes driving) from where you work. You might be surprised to see how many areas are suitable.

Then, when you have time in the evening of this day or the next, call on a few ads that look appealing, or drive through areas you find interesting to see what neighborhoods interest you. Remember, you might not find the house of your dreams the first time out, or the second, or the third. This could be a long process, so get started and continue as you have time.

First Weekend—Begin Fixing Up Your Existing Home

It's the rare property that will sell without some cleaning and repair. You may need to paint at least the front of your home. Your yard will need sprucing up at the least, perhaps even a new lawn and shrubs in the front. Does your driveway need to be resurfaced?

These kinds of projects can best be done on the weekends, or whenever you have time off from work. Do it yourself and you'll save a bundle. But, you have to have time to do it; unless you get started now, you'll find you won't have time later on.

Remember, just as Rome wasn't built in a day, you probably won't be able to get your house ready in a weekend. Use your first days to assess what needs to be done. Then come up with a separate plan for getting it done. For clues on accomplishing this, see Chapter 5.

Within Three Weeks—
Look for an Agent Who Will Work with You

You'll be contacting many agents as you look at houses, so this will come almost naturally. You'll want to interview them much as you would interview anyone else you were hiring.

You'll want to make sure they are compatible with you. You don't want an agent who is too pushy, or too laid back. You want someone who can get the job done, find a new home for you, and sell the old one.

You also want to ascertain up front that the agent is willing to discount his or her commission for a double buy-sell transaction. It may take some time to find this agent. For hints on finding the right agent, see Chapter 6.

Within Six Weeks—List Your Home

You can't sell your home until you list it, or put it up for sale "by owner" (FSBO). You also don't want to list it until it's ready to be shown. One of the biggest mistakes you can make is to list the property when it's still in a shoddy condition. You're just asking for lowball offers when you do this.

You want to fix your home and list it as soon as possible. But, you don't want to kill yourself doing this. If you're fixing it up on weekends, six weeks is reasonable to aim for. For listing tips, see Chapter 6.

As Soon as Possible—Make an Offer on Another Home

Don't make the mistake of thinking you must wait until you sell before you buy. You can buy before you sell. And if you find the home of your dreams, you want to tie it up as quickly as possible before it gets away. For clues on how to do this, see Chapter 7.

As Soon as You Get a Deal—
Begin Working on Your Moving Plans

It can take weeks, sometimes months, to line up movers, at least the good ones who will do it for a reasonable price and not break too much. If you wait until everything closes and you're ready to move, you'll only get the leftovers.

Call movers. Also, check into temporary storage as well as a place to stay in case both homes don't close simultaneously. If you plan early, you can arrange to stay with friends, relatives, or in low-cost long-term housing, instead of in a high-priced motel.

You'll also want to get started addressing certain technical matters as soon as possible. These include checking out the sellers' disclosure statements, getting a home inspection, and moving forward with financing. For tips on closing the deal, see Chapter 9.

Before the Deal Closes—Recheck Everything

Make sure your loan documentation is in hand, your moving plans are finalized, and your deposit has been given. You'll also want to be sure you've completed other plans, such as arranging for a new school for the children, calling up for utilities, cashing in bonds or mutual funds to make sure you'll have cash on hand, and so on. For hints on getting this done, see Chapters 8 and 9.

It Isn't Difficult

These are a lot of balls to keep in the air at once, but the round-trip real estate transaction is far from impossible. And once you get into it, you'll find that it's far easier than you imagined. What's important is to get started.

Take Direct Action

Many great ideas get lost due to inaction. Each of us during our lifetimes can cite turning points where, if we had only taken decisive action, things might have worked out differently (sometimes better, sometimes worse). No matter how committed you are to selling your existing home and buying a new one, it's all daydreaming until you actually take action. By moving on the nonlinear time line we discussed, you actually put a plan into action, get started, and show your spouse and even yourself that you really mean to do what you say you want to do.

Selling and Buying Take Time—Don't Waste It

In most markets, you won't find the house you want, at the price you want, immediately. And you won't be able to sell your house the day you list it, or the week or even the month. It takes time, sometimes lots of time, perhaps as long as three to six months or even more.

By getting preapproved for financing, looking for a new home, fixing up your old one, listing it, and making other preparations, you get a head start on the process that ultimately will net you a new home. Waiting is nothing more than wasting time—something you won't be doing.

The Checklist: Buy-Sell Juggling Act
• •

❏ 1. Day one—Get started on your loan preapproval.

❏ 2. Day two—Start looking for a new home.

❏ 3. First weekend—Begin fixing up your existing home.

❏ 4. Within three weeks—Look for an agent who will work with you.

❏ 5. Within six weeks—List your existing home.

❏ 6. As soon as possible—Make an offer on another home.

❏ 7. As soon as you get a deal—Begin working on your moving plans.

❏ 8. Before the deal closes—Recheck everything.

Day One: Getting Preapproved for Financing

The first step you need to take in the buy-sell juggling act introduced in Chapter 2, is to get preapproved for financing.

Financing? you may ask, I haven't even begun looking for my next house, let alone sold the old one. Isn't it a bit early for financing? After all, I could spend this valuable time looking for a new home or getting my existing home ready for resale!

Why Get Preapproved First?

The reason to put loan preapproval first is that you don't know when you'll find the property you want to buy. You could find it in three or six months—or tomorrow. But no matter when you do, you want to be able to act immediately. And preapproval gives you leverage when you act.

Three big questions must be answered when obtaining a mortgage:

1. How big a loan can I get?
2. What kind of a loan will it be?
3. Will I actually qualify for any loan?

In the old days, a mortgage borrower never really knew the answers to the big three until the offer was accepted and the mortgage had been applied for.

It could take a month or more to get loan approval, which may come just a few days before escrow closes and the deal is completed. Thus, the most important factor affecting a person's ability to make a purchase was not known until the very last minute. If there was a credit problem or if the buyer didn't qualify in some other way, no one would know it until it was too late to do anything about it (at least in terms of saving the existing deal). And the would-be buyer who had already committed to sell the old home could very quickly be out on the street with no place to live and a lot of furniture to move!

That's all changed in the last decade or so. A few years ago, most buyers who made offers on properties had been "qualified" in one way or another. This meant that someone had told them they had enough income and good enough credit to get the mortgages they were looking for. In many cases these buyers had a letter attesting to their qualifications, which they would often show, hoping to impress sellers.

·H·I·N·T ···

One of the most important reasons for getting preapproved is that you can demonstrate to a seller that you will be able to secure financing. This puts you way ahead of a competing buyer who can't demonstrate this ability. In some cases, it can even be used to leverage a lower price or lower terms, as we'll see shortly.

What Does It Mean to Be "Qualified"?

Being qualified means someone believes you are likely to get real estate financing. For several years, buyers used statements of qualifications to demonstrate to sellers that they were good candidates for home purchases.

The problem is that this qualification is nothing more than a statement of opinion you can get from anyone. The letter simply states that someone, who presumably has looked at your income and credit, has determined, based on what they know about mortgage lending, that you should be able to get a loan. Your real estate agent can give you a qualifying letter. Or your mortgage broker. Or your Aunt Hilda from Brisbane. Or even you, yourself. And as we'll discuss later, many online wizards can walk you through the basics of qualifying.

This letter really is not worth much more than the paper it's written on. It says that when you apply for a mortgage, you are likely to get it. In short, it's just a preamble, a preface, to actually applying for and getting approval. It's not something you should risk a transaction on. (And savvy sellers these days won't.) It's not good enough for you to use to commit yourself to selling your old home, let alone buying a new one. In some ways it's worse than nothing, because if it's incorrect, it can lead to unsound real estate decisions.

What Is a True Preapproval?

A qualification is a statement of opinion; preapproval is a statement of fact. By preapproving you, a true lender says that you not only can get a mortgage, you've got one. All you need is a property to use for collateral.

To obtain preapproval, you go through the process of applying for a mortgage—you fill out an application, put up the $50 or so for a complete (three-bureau) credit report, get underwriting approval, and have a lender who's ready to fund. It's roughly equivalent to a letter of credit from a commercial bank (except, with a credit letter, no collateral is usually required). In other words, you've got a lender standing behind you, virtually ready to fund the money.

A true preapproval letter can be a mighty force in shaping your future moves. It lets you know that not only can you get a mortgage on a new home, but you know your maximum mortgage amount. In other words, it tells you how big a new home you can afford.

It's also heavy artillery when motivating sellers. If they sell to you, subject to whatever contingencies are in the contract, the sale is a "done deal." You're a sure-thing buyer.

I've been at presentations with sellers in hot markets when two or three offers have come in simultaneously. Typically in cases like these, the offers are all for full price or more. (The buyers know they are in competition with one another and are trying to make the top offer to get the property.) If only one of these buyers has a preapproval letter, while others only have "qualified" letters, the preapproval letter often holds sway, sometimes even if the offer is for slightly less!

In other circumstances, sellers who are anxious to sell quickly will accept less than their asking price if the buyers have a preapproval letter. They feel assured the deal will go through with a minimum of hassles in a very short time.

In short, getting a preapproval letter is a must if you want to be assured you can move ahead with a buy-sell. And it's a must if you want to have the best chance of getting the property you want at the most favorable price and terms.

Why Do It Right Away?

Unlike a letter that qualifies you, which can be typed out in a few minutes, a preapproval letter takes time. The lender has to check your application, check your credit, perhaps get verification of employment and deposit of funds (your down payment) from a bank. Then it has to all be submitted to an underwriter. (For most loans, these are Federal National Mortgage Association, or "Fannie Mae," or Federal Home Loan Mortgage Corporation, or "Freddie Mac," for approval.) Only when this is complete will the lender issue the preapproval letter. This can take anywhere from a few days (for electronic approval) to six weeks or more if there's some problem that you must correct.

Get started early; obtaining a preapproval letter could take longer than you expect. You never know what problems could arise when you attempt to secure mortgage financing. If you start now, chances are you'll have the letter in hand by the time you make your offer.

·H·I·N·T ·

A lender may issue a preliminary preapproval letter after you've completed your application and credit report, but before underwriting approval is obtained. This letter usually states that you are approved subject to underwriting or some other factor. It is a lesser quality letter, but may serve if you are short of time.

What Problems Could Crop Up?

Anything can happen. A few years ago I was applying for a mortgage and a credit check revealed my name was still on a mortgage for a Phoenix property I had sold years before. Apparently the escrow company handling the transaction had failed to transfer the name on the mortgage to the party who had assumed it. As far as the lender was concerned, I was still liable for making payments on that old loan, which affected my ability to qualify for payments on the new mortgage. I had to contact the escrow company in Phoenix, have them properly execute assumption documents, and get the old lender to process them before the old mortgage could be taken off my credit report. The entire process took several months.

Of course, it could be something less esoteric. A credit check might turn up unpaid bills, late payments, or a previous foreclosure or bankruptcy. Presumably, you would have been aware of all these, but sometimes not. There could be a mistake in names. Or the lender might not know that a bill had been paid off.

The problem could be that you don't have enough income to warrant the mortgage amount you are seeking, at least in the eye of the lender (which, after all, are the only eyes that count here). Or perhaps the lender wants you to put 20 percent down instead of the 10 percent you are planing to put down. You might have to produce evidence of other income, or switch lenders to get a more favorable down payment amount.

·**H**·**I**·**N**·**T**· ·

This is a good argument for checking your credit on a regular basis. Three national credit bureaus handle real estate financing:

Experian (formerly TRW)	800-682-7654
Trans Union	800-916-8800
Equifax	800-685-1111

Any of these will offer to check your own credit for a nominal fee, usually under $10. It is money well spent. When a mortgage lender looks over your credit, it gets a three-bureau check that looks into all of the above.

In short, the problems that could arise, and often do, are endless. And you won't know about them until you actually apply for the mortgage. (Which is one of the big reasons that sellers are so worried about buyers who don't have preapproval letters.)

What Other Considerations Apply with a Preapproval?

When you apply for preapproval, you'll be asked a number of questions such as, "How big a mortgage do you want?" "Do you want a conforming loan?" "Will you accept an adjustable interest rate?" and so on.

You need to be able to answer these questions in such a way that will get the best mortgage for you. Of course, you can always ask the mortgage broker what the best mortgage is for you, but he or she is going to be busy and, at best, is likely only to give you a very superficial answer. Therefore, for the remainder of this chapter, we'll go into the choices you need to make when getting preapproved.

How Big a Mortgage Will I Need?

If you don't have a house in mind, you don't know exactly how big a mortgage to go for. For example, if the house is $200,000 and you're putting 10 percent down, you'll need a $180,000 loan. But, if the house is $300,000 and you're putting 10 percent down, you'll need much more, $270,000.

When you apply for preapproval, you'll be asked how big a mortgage you want.

How much should you go for? The answer is easy. Go for the most you can get. Apply for a sky-high loan. The mortgage company will then tell you the maximum for which you'll be preapproved.

·H·I·N·T ·

When you actually make an offer on a property, it's usually a good idea to get a preapproval letter that specifies no more than the mortgage amount needed to complete the deal. If you need $240,000 to make the deal and the letter says you are preapproved for $260,000, the sellers are going to come back with a higher counteroffer. They'll say that because you can borrow more, you should, and the difference should go to them in the form of a higher price!

The amount for which you are preapproved, the time it takes to get the mortgage, and your monthly payments now and in the future, also depend on the interest rate at the time you apply, as well as the type of mortgage you apply for. Let's consider the most common mortgage types.

What Is a Conforming Loan?

If you are aiming to buy a moderate- to low-priced property, you'll probably want to first try for a "conforming" loan, which usually offers the lowest interest rate and mortgage payments.

· **H** · **I** · **N** · **T** ·

Conforming mortgages have a maximum loan amount, which changes occasionally. As of this writing the maximum amount is $240,000, which is why they are used primarily for moderate to low-cost housing.

Conforming means that the mortgage meets the underwriting standards of the two largest secondary lenders in the country, Fannie Mae and Freddie Mac. These semipublic corporations buy the loan from the primary lender, who lends it to you. For example, if you get a loan from XYZ mortgage company, that company will "sell" the loan to Freddie Mac or Fannie Mae and recoup the money it loaned you, so that it can relend it to someone else. (The primary lender also will get a small percentage of the interest and the ability to service the mortgage for a fee.)

Before loans can be sold to Freddie Mac or Fannie Mae, the borrowers must conform to those secondary lenders' specifications, which means you must meet a specific credit profile. Meet the profile and the mortgage is yours. Don't meet it and you can't get it.

Okay, you may wonder, so what's the profile? It's a complicated set of requirements that only the secondary lenders know. They won't release the information, lest borrowers tailor their applications to meet the profile.

Widely known to be part of the profile is your "credit score." Your credit report is data, a listing of your paid and late bills and other credit information. It needs to be interpreted in order to give the secondary lender a sense of whether you're a good credit risk. Several companies nationwide interpret credit reports, the largest of which is Fair Isaac, which offers a FICO rating between 300 and 900 points. Usually you need a score of around 660 or better to get a conforming loan.

If you have a good FICO credit score, enough income to make the payments, as determined by the secondary lender's arcane profile, you'll get a conforming loan. If you don't, you won't. For more information on profiles and scoring, read *Get an Instant Mortgage,* by Irwin and Ganz (New York: John Wiley & Sons, 1997).

What Is a Jumbo Loan?

In many parts of the country, particularly along the coasts and in Alaska and Hawaii, properties cost more than can be financed with a conforming loan. If you're in this situation, how do you get financing? What kind of preapproval do you look for?

The answer is the "jumbo" loan. Generally speaking, any mortgage for more than the maximum conforming loan amount is considered a jumbo. There's virtually no maximum amount for a jumbo loan, although different lenders impose their own limitations. One lender may offer jumbos to $600,000, another to $1.3 million, yet another to $2 million. If you're fortunate to be able to purchase a house in this jumbo category, you'll want to seek a mortgage broker who can direct you to high-end lenders.

A jumbo loan typically carries a higher interest rate than a conforming loan, usually by a half point or more. Because of this higher interest rate, lenders are looking for people to lend jumbos to.

Generally speaking, a lender who offers a jumbo will not sell that mortgage on the secondary market, but will instead keep it in its own portfolio of loans. Hence, jumbos are also sometimes referred to as "portfolio" loans.

Because of their large size, it takes a big lender to be able to afford to offer jumbos. However, it is possible to combine a jumbo with a conforming loan so that the lender doesn't have to offer so much of its own money on a long-term basis. These are sometimes called "piggy-back" loans.

Here, a lender offers a conforming loan up to the maximum limit and then a jumbo on top of that, up to the amount you may want. For example, if you want $400,000, there might be a conforming loan for $240,000 and a piggyback for $160,000, for a total of $400,000. The combined interest rate would be lower than for a straight jumbo, because it would be a blend of the lower conforming rate and the higher jumbo rate. As a borrower, you would make only one payment to the lender, who would sell the conforming loan on the secondary market and make payments to it while keeping the balance of your monthly payment to cover the piggyback amount. The interest rate also would be lower than for a straight jumbo.

Jumbos are readily available where needed in most high-priced markets. But you must ask for them and go to a lender who offers them.

Should I Always Get a Fixed-Rate Loan?

The fixed-rate mortgage, where the interest rate does not fluctuate for the entire term of the loan (typically 30 years), is the mortgage of choice for most people. It's what you generally ask for when you see a lender.

But it might not always be your best choice, particularly if you're having trouble qualifying for a big enough mortgage on your preapproval. How big a mortgage you can get depends on your income and your expenses. A lower income, or higher expenses, may keep you from getting a big enough fixed-rate mortgage. If that's the case, consider some of the alternatives.

What Is a Balloon 7/30 Mortgage?

One popular alternative is the balloon mortgage, which offers a lower interest rate and, consequently, a lower monthly payment. In its most common form, the payments are amortized (paid out equally) over its 30-year term. Before 30 years, you have a balloon payment in which all of the remaining principal is due. Typically this is at year seven, although it could be at any time. Other common due dates are at years three, five, and ten.

Here's how it works: Say you are applying for a mortgage of $100,000 for 30 years at 7.5 percent interest. Your payments, if the mortgage were fully amortized, would be $699 a month. However, let's say you were willing to accept a balloon payment at the end of year seven. That means you would make 83 payments of $699 a month and then one last payment where the entire balance of the mortgage was due. (Presumably before that time you would resell or refinance the property.)

For the lender, this seven-year due date is much better than a 30-year due date. It means the money will come back much sooner and there's far less time during which interest rate fluctuations could undermine the loan's value. Therefore, the lender is usually willing to give a concession in the interest rate, say half a point. Thus, now you get a 7 percent mortgage that works out to $665 a month, or a savings of $35 a month. If you get an even shorter balloon, the cut in interest rate would be steeper, a longer balloon and it would be less.

Now you make payments of $665 a month for seven years, before the mortgage comes due. When you're in a crunch to get enough money or to keep your payments down, this type of mortgage can be a real lifesaver.

What Is an Adjustable-Rate Mortgage?

This mortgage became popular during the late 1970s and early 1980s when interest rates were in the double digits. Here your interest rate fluctuates according to the interest rate market in general. Your rate is tied to an index of other rates, such as the overall mortgage interest rate, the 30-year bond, or any of a dozen other rates. As they go up or down, so too does your mortgage rate, and correspondingly, so do your monthly payments. (The actual calculation involves both the index and a margin added by the lender.)

There are as many different types of adjustable-rate mortgages as you can shake a stick at. They involve controlling the following:

- Adjustment periods—how often your mortgage interest rate is raised or lowered
- Steps—how big an adjustment can be made each period
- Caps—the maximum the interest rate, mortgage payment, or both can be adjusted each period

The big pluses with an adjustable-rate mortgage is that, because the interest rate is able to adjust to market conditions relatively quickly, there is less risk to the lender than from a fixed-rate loan. Hence, the interest rate is often much lower, at least initially.

On the other hand, the initial low interest rate (called a "teaser rate") often quickly goes up once you get the mortgage. Hence, you could end up paying as much, sometimes more, than for a fixed-rate mortgage.

Further, with payment caps you could get "negative amortization." Here, you end up keeping your payments low, but adding accrued interest to the principal of your mortgage. You could end up owing more than your starting balance!

And there's also the fact that you never know for sure what your monthly payment will be. If interest rates go up, it will likewise go up. If they go down, it will drop.

When Should I Get an Adjustable and When a Fixed?

The general rule is to get preapproved for a fixed-rate mortgage when interest rates are low, thus locking in a low rate. Go for an adjustable mortgage when rates are high (you get a lower initial interest rate and a lower initial monthly payment) and when rates eventually fall, so, too will your mortgage interest rate and payment. Further, it may pay to get an adjustable-rate mortgage when you plan to resell quickly. You thus take advantage of the low initial rate and sell before the interest rate and monthly payments can rise.

What Other Kinds of Mortgages Are Available?

The possibilities are limited only by lenders' imaginations. There are mortgages specifically for self-employed people, for those who have no credit, for those who have large assets, for those who are prime borrowers, and on and on.

For more information on the different loans available, I suggest you read my book, *Tips and Traps When Mortgage Hunting,* 2nd edition (New York: McGraw-Hill, 1999).

What about Prepayment Penalties?

I would be remiss if I didn't mention an ugly old phenomenon that is having a rebirth, the prepayment penalty. I suggest that before applying with any lender you ask if their loans have prepayment penalties. If they do, I suggest you go elsewhere. Many, many lenders offer financing with no such penalty.

A prepayment penalty simply means that you agree to pay the lender a penalty if you pay off the mortgage early. In the old days, this meant any time before the loan's due date, even if that were 30 years off. Today, it usually means within five years of getting the loan.

Lenders want a prepayment penalty to keep you from going out and refinancing only a short time after you get the mortgage from them, something borrowers frequently do when interest rates are falling. It costs the lender time and money to reshelf the loan money and then find and reloan it. They'd rather you just kept making payments.

On the other hand, from your perspective, refinancing makes perfectly good sense. Why keep making payments on a 7.5 percent mortgage when rates have fallen to 6 percent? Just refinance and pay less each month.

Again, just say no when it comes to the prepayment penalty.

Where Do I Go to Get a Mortgage?

The following are among the many sources of mortgages in this country:

- Banks
- Savings and loans
- Credit unions
- Mortgage brokers
- Mortgage bankers

In today's market, the mortgage broker is probably your best source of real estate financing. Today, rather than open expensive storefronts, advertise, and hire staffs in many different areas, lenders prefer to "wholesale" their loans to mortgage brokers. Mortgage brokers are like department stores; they "retail" mortgages to you, the consumer, for a variety of lenders.

When you work with a mortgage broker, you pay retail price for your loan. To stay in business, the mortgage brokers have to make a profit, so they pay wholesale, and mark up the "price" of the loan— paid by the lender to the mortgage broker, not directly by you— a small amount, usually around 1 percent of the loan.

A good mortgage broker can offer you mortgages from dozens, sometimes hundreds, of different lenders, from banks to insurance companies from down the street or across the country. While you can go from bank to bank and savings and loan to savings and loan and ask what their mortgage programs are, the far easier method is to consult with a couple of mortgage brokers. They will be happy to offer you multiple loan programs. Further, if you tell them what you are specifically looking for, they can often pick the best lender for your needs.

A mortgage broker is usually a real estate agent licensed by the state to deal in mortgages. He or she typically has a sophisticated knowledge of real estate financing and has specialized in mortgages for a long time.

You can find mortgage brokers listed in the yellow pages of the phone book. Real estate agents and friends can probably recommend you to brokers with whom they had good experiences.

But be careful, unscrupulous mortgage brokers (a very few) can cause you harm. I would never pay a fee in advance, with the exception of around $50 for a credit report and around $300 for an appraisal when I've found my home. Advance fees, even when they are applied to the mortgage costs later on, simply lock you into the broker and keep you from shopping around.

When shopping for a mortgage broker the same rules apply as would when seeking a real estate agent. Check out references. Get an active broker who works with lots of lenders. Compare interest rates and terms on the mortgages.

What Is a Mortgage Banker?

A mortgage banker makes mortgage loans, like a regular bank or savings and loan. However, while a regular bank or savings and loan offers consumer services such as checking and savings accounts, safety deposit boxes, commercial loans, and so forth, the mortgage banker only has one function—to make real estate loans.

Some of the country's largest independent lenders are mortgage bankers and deal directly with consumers. Others, seldom heard of, deal exclusively at wholesale with mortgage brokers.

Don't expect to save any money by dealing with a mortgage broker. It's a very competitive business, margins are tight, and there are few discounts. The exception here is when borrowing online.

Can I Get Preapproved Using the Internet?

Yes, and you can get some of the best financing available, although at present most online preapproval is limited to conforming loans as explained earlier.

To get real estate financing on the Internet, you must have the usual setup—a computer, a modem, and an ISP (Internet service provider) such as AOL (America Online), MSN (Microsoft Network), or some other service. If you're not sure how to get all of this, simply check at any store where computers are sold. They can provide you with free, easy-to-install-and-understand software. (Most modern computers already come with built-in high-speed modems.)

Once you're online, simply go to the Web and enter the screen address of a mortgage lender. Following are some of the best as of this writing:

- www.eloan.com
- www.chase.com
- www.homeshark.com
- www.homefair.com
- www.namc.com
- www.mortgage.quicken.com

Virtually all of the loan sites include calculators that allow you to input the mortgage interest rate and term and then spit out your monthly payment. Most also include "wizards," into which you can enter your critical financial information and out of which you will be given recommendations for the types of loans to get. The calculators are uniformly excellent. The wizards, in my experience, mostly leave a lot to be desired.

·**H**·**I**·**N**·**T** ·

Be sure to check for "garbage costs." These are incidentals thrown in that can amount to thousands in extra mortgage costs. Don't shop just for interest rate and monthly payment, or you could get hit with a frighteningly huge garbage-cost payment at closing. For more information on "garbage costs," see Chapter 9.

Most online brokers allow you to apply for a mortgage. They collect a nominal fee for processing a credit report and then handle the underwriting. Many will offer to send you by e-mail, fax, or regular mail a letter of preapproval once you're fairly along in the process.

What Is the Advantage of Using the Internet?

One of the biggest bonuses is the discount. Internet loans are not true retailed mortgages; they are somewhere between retail and wholesale. (Neither the retailer who runs the Web site nor the wholesale lender who offers the mortgage has much in the way of costs.) For that reason, you can often get a discount, sometimes as much as ½ to 1 percent of the loan amount. In addition, some Internet lenders will offer to reimburse you for the costs of both the appraisal and the credit report, if you follow through and eventually get the mortgage from them.

But it's not all peaches and cream. Sometimes lenders over the Internet can take a long time to fund, which can jeopardize your deal. In other cases they can make promises they can't deliver. And then there's the paperwork. While much can be done electronically and by fax, at some point you do have to go into an office and meet with the lender (or an escrow officer) to present your documentation and sign the loan agreement.

Nevertheless, electronic lending is definitely the wave of the future. Within a decade it may be the only way to get a mortgage! For more information on getting a loan over the internet, check out my book, *Buying a Home on the Internet,* (New York: McGraw-Hill, 1999).

The Quiz: Getting Preapproved for Financing

Yes　No

❏　❏　　1. Can anyone qualify you for a mortgage?

❏　❏　　2. Can only a bank tell you how big a loan you can get?

❏　❏　　3. Should you wait until you find a new home to get preapproved?

❏　❏　　4. Can a mortgage broker arrange for preapproval?

❏　❏　　5. Is it true that only a true lender can preapprove you?

❏　❏　　6. Can credit problems only surface after you apply for a mortgage?

❏　❏　　7. Should you get a credit report on yourself?

❏　❏　　8. Should you automatically apply for the biggest mortgage you can get?

❏　❏　　9. Should you take out the biggest mortgage you can get?

❏　❏　10. Is a conforming loan one that fits neatly into a 8½″ × 11″ inch folder?

❏　❏　11. Can a mortgage broker get you a conforming loan?

❏　❏　12. Can only a prime borrower qualify for a conforming loan?

❏　❏　13. Is a jumbo loan one that is used in circuses?

❏ ❏ 14. Is a piggyback loan a combination of jumbo and port-folio mortgages?

❏ ❏ 15. Can a piggyback loan offer a lower interest rate?

❏ ❏ 16. Is a fixed-rate loan always the best kind to get?

❏ ❏ 17. Should an adjustable-rate loan be locked in when interest rates are low?

❏ ❏ 18. Does a 7/30 loan combine a balloon payment with a 30-year amortized mortgage?

❏ ❏ 19. Is a mortgage banker a direct lender?

❏ ❏ 20. Can I get a discount on my mortgage by using the Internet?

Answers

1. They sure can, and that's why just being "qualified" usually is meaningless.
2. You can get an educated guess from any number of people, including mortgage brokers, agents, and online lenders, but only a lender can tell you for sure.
3. No. Get preapproved right now, before you even start looking. It may even help you get a better deal.
4. Yes, they can, but usually they can't preapprove you themselves; only a lender can do that.
5. Yes, exactly.
6. The credit problems are there. They only show up after you apply for credit.
7. It's a good way to find out if there are any hidden problems that could affect your ability to get financing.
8. It's probably a good idea to apply for the biggest loan. Remember, you don't have to take it all.

9. That depends on whether you feel you can handle the payments. (Just because a lender says you can, doesn't mean you'll feel comfortable. Remember, the lender isn't the one who has to make the monthly dole.)

10. Sure, and a FSBO is mint candy. A conforming loan conforms to the underwriting requirements of the two big secondary lenders, Freddie Mac or Fannie Mae.

11. Yes, he or she can, if they're any good and you qualify.

12. Conforming loans normally go to only the best, or to prime borrowers. However, there are many exceptions depending on the profile used by the secondary lenders.

13. While it may be as big as an elephant, it's not in circuses. It means any loan above the conforming maximum limit.

14. Yes, it is. It's two loans in one, although you only make one payment.

15. Yes, it can, by blending a lower interest rate conforming mortgage with a higher interest rate portfolio loan.

16. Not when interest rates are high. An adjustable may make more sense for you at that time.

17. Just the opposite. "Lock in" low interest rates with a fixed-rate loan. The adjustable rate doesn't lock in a rate, it adjusts.

18. Yes, and it's one of the most popular because it gives you a 30-year loan payment with a shorter-term interest rate.

19. Yes, a mortgage banker lends its own money, but many do not deal directly with consumers.

20. Many legitimate Internet lenders offer discounts to borrowers at least as of this writing.

4

Day Two: Locating Your Next Home

Once you've made the decision to sell your home and move to another, and have begun the loan preapproval process, my advice to you is to immediately start looking for your new property. As we saw in Chapter 2, it's all a juggling act, and one of the balls to keep in the air is the search for the new home. This is not something to delay, but rather a first priority.

But, you may be asking, isn't is risky to look first, and even financially dangerous to buy before selling my old home?

Why Should I Look for the Next Home First?

The conventional wisdom is that you should wait until you sell your existing home before looking for and buying your next one. The reasons are obvious. It isn't until after your sale is complete that you know for sure that you've got a buyer and how much money you'll get. In other words, waiting is supposedly the "safe" course.

I disagree. Assuming the market is liquid, that is, that there are ongoing sales of homes in your area, your chances of selling, assuming a decent well-priced home, are virtually certain. You will sell your home, eventually.

Further, you can make an accurate estimate of how long it will take to sell. By checking with a broker (as described in Chapter 6) you can quickly learn the average time between listing and sale of properties in your area. It might be a week, a month, 60 days, or whatever. Assuming you price your home right and fix it so it shows well (which we'll go into in great detail in Chapter 5), that's about how long it will take to sell. (Don't forget to add in the extra 30 days or so for closing.)

But is it really the safer course?

Again, I believe it often is. In an active rising market, prices of homes you'll want to buy (as well as the one you're selling) are advancing. That means that any delays you impose yourself will only result in a higher price to pay later on. If you delay six months and housing prices are moving up 5 percent a year, you're going to have to spend 2½ percent more to buy the same house. That may not seem like much until you realize that on a $200,000 price that's an additional $5,000. Wouldn't it be so much better to tie up that next house now?

Further, if you wait a bit to sell your existing home, you can take advantage of any price increases. You might be able to get more for your house just by delaying a bit. (Of course, the opposite would be true in a falling market.)

Are There Side Benefits of Looking for a Home First?

There certainly are, two big ones. As you check out homes to buy, particularly those close to where you currently live, you quickly get educated as to what the market is doing. Chances are some of those homes you are looking at will be in competition with your existing home when you list and sell. As you check out the competition, you'll get a much better feel for how much you can sell your home for, and how to deal with buyers and agents.

A Realistic Asking Price

Most homeowners feel they have a sense for the real estate market. Because you're invested in property, chances are you read articles about rising or falling housing prices (naturally you want to see how homes in your area are doing). When a neighbor sells a home, most of us tend to ask around to see how much the seller got. Even at parties when the topic turns to real estate, each of us tends to put in our two cents worth about where the market's heading and what property values are.

The truth, however, is that very few people have accurate knowledge of where the real estate market is at any given moment. Instead, we rely on gossip and rumors. This can do us great harm when we decide to move because we may be totally off base in thinking we can even afford another home!

Remember that the price you can get for your home has very little to do with what you want or need from your property. Rather, it's what the market will bear. That's what you'll very quickly come to see as you begin to look for a new house.

Dealing with Buyers and Agents

As you conduct your home search, you'll come in contact with many sellers and agents. You'll form impressions of how you were treated and what kind of conduct worked best. Thus, when the roles are reversed and you're the seller, you can talk to potential buyers in a way they will appreciate. And you'll have a better sense of what you're looking for in a broker.

Where Should I Look For My Next Home?

Once you've decided to start looking, the next logical question is, where? Should you look close to home or far afield? Where you look is determined, at least at first, by your motivation to move. Why don't you want to stay where you are?

- Is your existing home too small? If so, you'll want to look in an area of larger homes.
- Are you retired and feel your home is too big? Then you'll want to look for more modestly sized properties.

- Are you concerned about the neighborhood's deterioration? Then a better neighborhood will be your primary concern. (Location should always be a main concern when buying real estate.)
- Are you being transferred? Then, of course, you'll want to look in the area to which you're being relocated.

It really doesn't matter where you start looking, because sooner or later prices, home dimensions, neighborhood quality, and other factors of concern to you will direct you to the right area. However, to help get started, consider the following resources.

Search for Your Next Home Online

There are at least a half dozen great sources of home listings with more than a million homes listed nationwide. The properties are listed by area, but some services also allow you to search by number of bedrooms and baths or by square footage or by price.

All you need is a computer, a modem, and an Internet service provider. Access one of these services on the Internet and check out the following home listings:

- yahoo.com—Homes listed by agents and for sale by owners are listed.
- realtor.com—This site features properties listed by agents in many areas.
- cyberhome.com—This site features homes listed by agents.

Drive Neighborhoods

You may already have an idea of where you'd like to live. If so, drive through the area. Is its appearance all that you anticipated? (It may not be. Sometimes we remember a particular neighborhood with warmth because an old friend used to live there or because we used to be familiar with it years ago. But today it may be quite different and not nearly as desirable as we remembered.)

You are bound to find homes listed by agents or by owners. Call on these to see what's on the market right now.

Should the Listing Agent Show Me the New Home?

As soon as you begin your housing search, you'll discover that almost everything is listed. And in order to see the listing, you'll need to be accompanied by a broker. This presents some very specific problems for round-trip buyer-sellers.

Have you experienced this scenario? You're traveling a neighborhood and see a house that looks like something you want—only it's listed. So you call up the listing office, get an agent on the line and, before you can snap your fingers, that agent is down there showing it to you.

Here's the problem: If an agent shows you a property, you may be committed to working with that agent if you decide to buy that property. Other agents might not be able to get a full commission on that particular house; the agent who first showed it to you may have it locked in for at least a part commission. This could have important ramifications when it comes to listing your existing house and cutting a deal for a reduced commission.

If you like the agent and find he or she is knowledgeable, effective, and straight as an arrow, going with the listing agent may be great. On the other hand, real estate brokerage is a highly competitive business and, while the majority of agents do a good job, some do not. You've just taken the luck of the draw and the agent you got may not have a personality that works well with you, or may be less honest than you'd like.

It's most important that you find an agent you like, who meets your expectations for competency and honesty, and who realizes that, because you're a round-trip buyer-seller, you're entitled to a break on the commission. When you find this agent, have him or her show you the property. We'll discuss how to find such an agent in Chapter 6.

Check Out New Homes

Perhaps your motivation is to buy new. If so, then check out any new subdivisions in your area. All of them will have model homes you can walk through to see what the builders are putting up.

·H·I·N·T· ·

If you walk through a model home and sign in, then later on if you decide to buy, you'll probably have to buy through the builder. Real estate agents probably won't be able to get a commission on the deal because they didn't show you the new home first. This could affect your ability to negotiate a lower round-trip commission when you sell your existing home.

New home prices are not the same as the prices for resales. In a sense, it's a wholly different market, with prices determined by current land and building costs. (Resales were established originally in the same way, but have moved up—or down—as market conditions have changed.) This means that if you only visit new model homes, you'll get a skewed sense of where the market for resales is. By looking only at new, you may come to believe that the resale market (the far larger market) is either much higher or lower than it really is. All of which is to say, check out both new and resales.

Don't Forget to Look in Gated and Specialized Communities

In general, if the neighborhood has gates, its home prices will be at least 5 percent higher than the prices of homes outside the gates. That works both ways: You'll have to pay more when you buy; but you'll also get more when you sell. In a time of great national concern over crime and personal safety, many buyers are willing to pay more for the perception of security that gates give. (It's not clear that gated communities are, in fact, actually more secure—it depends on other factors, including how alert to crime the neighbors are, and how close to high-crime areas the gated community is located.)

Retirees often want to live in specialized adults-only communities. Generally these restrict the majority (or sometimes all) of the owners by an age limit, often 55 years. These communities may be composed of single-family dwellings or condominiums, but often they have community recreational facilities such as golf courses, tennis courts, and card rooms. If your goal is to downsize, a local retirement community may be for you.

Don't Overlook Homes a Great Distance Away

Many people (mostly retirees) flock to the warm climate and easier living style of Florida. Many others opt for the dry heat of Arizona, particularly in the Phoenix area.

If this appeals to you, or if you are being relocated to another part of the country, it pays to take the time to go there and check out your new "adopted community." Moving a great distance away can be a wrenching experience, but it could be the best option, depending on your situation and desires.

How Do You Determine What You Can Afford?

An important part of the home search is to learn what you realistically can afford. If you think you already know this, you could be in for a big surprise. You may be able to afford much more, or much less, than you originally thought.

Sticker shock is often the biggest surprise to round-trip home buyer-sellers. If you've owned your existing home for some time, you could learn that in today's market, you can't even afford to buy the home in which you are currently living, let alone purchase another property! This can be the case if you bought some time ago when housing prices were much lower, because your income hasn't kept pace with inflation. It can also be the case if your income has dropped significantly in recent years. Or maybe you've taken out second mortgages or home equity loans and you simply don't have the equity in your property to transfer to a down payment on another home.

For whatever reason, it might turn out that regardless of what you want to do, you may not be able to purchase a new home. And if that's the case, you may suddenly find that you're quite content to stay where you are!

Are There Any Pitfalls in Looking for the Next Home First?

There's really only one big pitfall. You might find the house you want almost immediately! Now what do you do? You've located the house of your dreams, yet you haven't even begun to put your old home up for sale! Isn't this the perfect argument for selling your last home before looking for the next?

Don't become too alarmed. First of all, chances are it won't be that easy to find that perfect home. And even if you think you have, the ongoing search process may make you realize that it's not quite as perfect as you thought.

I still remember the first home my wife and I bought after we were married. We saw it once, made an offer, and had it accepted. Only later when we came back several times did we realize that the neighborhood wasn't nearly as good as we hoped, the home was actually not laid out as well as we liked and it had many features that, upon consideration, we found we didn't want. But, we had already sold our old home, had the money cash-in-hand and had been desperate to buy another place. So we jumped at the first seemingly close fit we found, and made a bit of a mistake. If we didn't have the pressure of needing a new home immediately, we wouldn't have bought so quickly and would have saved ourselves no small amount of headache and financial strain!

Besides, if, after due consideration (and many trips back), it does turn out to be your dream house, there are ways to lock it in before you sell your existing home, and ways to get your equity transferred to the next home even before you sell the old one. We'll explore these in Chapter 7.

The Quiz: House-Hunting

Yes   No

☐   ☐   1. Should you look for a new home before selling your old one?

☐   ☐   2. Will house-hunting bring you up to speed on the real estate market?

☐   ☐   3. Can you house-hunt in both a local and a distant area?

☐   ☐   4. Will checking out the market for a new home help you price and sell your existing home?

☐   ☐   5. Can you learn to deal with buyers by becoming a buyer yourself?

☐   ☐   6. Can looking at homes help you to find a good agent?

☐   ☐   7. Can there be problems with calling a new listing agent for each house you want to see?

☐   ☐   8. Can you search for a home online?

☐   ☐   9. Should you drive through neighborhoods when searching for a house?

☐   ☐   10. Should you look at new homes?

☐   ☐   11. Are gated communities usually worth the extra cost?

☐   ☐   12. If you find the home you like before selling your existing home, can you often buy it?

Answers

The yes answers obviously have it. If you find yourself answering no to any of the questions in this chapter's quiz, you may need to take a second look at the chapter text.

5

First Weekend: Fixing Up Your Home for a Quick Sale

It should go without saying that your existing home should be in tip-top shape if you want to sell it for a good price and do it quickly. Selling a home is like selling anything else—the better the product appears, the more enthused the buyers are going to be.

Can you imagine a used-car salesperson putting a car on the lot without first washing it, cleaning the upholstery, and fixing any nicks and dings? That salesperson wants potential buyers to see the car in its best light; that way they'll be willing to pay top dollar for it. Why should putting a house up for sale be any different?

No matter how wonderful you think your house may be, it can always use some fix-up work. Take the quiz at the end of the chapter to see what condition your home is really in.

In this chapter we're going to see how to accomplish the most at the least expense. But before we get to that, we're going to consider timing.

When Should You Begin Fixing Up Your Home for Resale?

In Chapter 2, I suggested you begin fixing up your home on the first available weekend. Why should this be such a priority? It has a lot to do with a common misconception: Most people assume that there's going to be very little to do to clean up their home—a few dabs of paint here, cleaning of a carpet or two, and washing off the driveway. Therefore, they wait until the last possible moment (which is just before they list it—or show it to buyers if they're going FSBO, or for sale by owner).

That's a mistake. Very often, particularly as your home gets older, there's a great deal of fix-up work to do, some of which can take a long time.

Consider the front lawn. The front lawn is important because it contributes to "curb appeal"—the first impression buyers get when seeing your property. As we all know, you only get one shot at making a good first impression. Therefore, the lawn becomes very important.

It takes a long time to grow a good lawn. It could take six months if you're starting from scratch with seed. If you're replanting, it could take a month or two. Even if you put in sod, you've got several weeks before it will begin to look appealing.

Other fix-ups also can take time. You may need to repaint the entire exterior of your home. Don't count on doing that in a couple of days. Or you may need to repaint the interior, replace some flooring, redo the ceiling or roof, or whatever. It all takes time. (Later in this chapter we'll look at how to schedule work to be done.)

Therefore, as soon as you decide to sell and buy a new home, it's time to begin fixing up your old one.

Should You Show Your Property before You Fix It Up?

The answer here is a definite no.

You never want to show your property until it's fixed up. Potential buyers simply won't see your home as it will look when all the work's done. Rather, they'll see it as it is now in its prefixed-up state. And, if they're not totally turned off, they'll make lowball offers. They'll discount the value of the fix-up work yet to be done. However, they won't just discount it at your cost. They'll discount it at what they think it might cost given any problems they might run into. Which is to say, for every dollar of work you see, chances are they'll see ten.

What If an Agent Wants to Show It before It's Ready?

Don't be coerced by an agent who insists on getting a listing signed right away. The agent may be afraid of losing the listing if you wait, or may be hungry for a commission. Take your time and do it right. That way you stand the best chance of getting the highest price, the best terms, and the fastest sale.

However, an agent may say, give me the listing and I won't put the property on the Multiple Listing Service. I'll just hold it until you're ready to show, but if any buyers come by, I can bring them around.

This is called keeping a "vest-pocket" listing. Besides being unethical, this may be against the rules of the MLS. Remember, any buyer is likely to offer less for a home that isn't ready to be shown. It doesn't matter whether that buyer is brought around by your agent or by someone else. Except in a super-hot market when any property will bring top dollar (and when, incidentally, you don't even need an agent to find a buyer!), there's no justification for showing until you're ready.

What Should I Do First?

Of course, we are putting the cart before the horse here, because we haven't really talked about what you need to do. Because time is always of the essence, here's what you should do in the order you should do them. Keep in mind, of course, that you may not need to do most of the items on this list.

·H·I·N·T ·

When you're fixing up your home, you should always do first that which will take the longest to accomplish.

Fix-Up Time Line

1. Apply for and obtain any necessary permits.
2. Hire contractors or workers as needed.
3. Do any yard excavation, soil leveling, or digging.
4. Plant shrubs and trees.
5. Plant or redo lawn.
6. Do any structural work, such as fixing the foundation, roof beams, changing interior walls, redoing the roof.
7. Do any remodeling, such as rebuilding the kitchen or a bathroom.
8. Do any repainting, outside first, then inside.
9. Replace carpet or flooring as needed. (If major floor replacement work is done, it should be accomplished before painting.)
10. Clean windows, tubs, showers, toilets, screens, and so on.

·**H**·**I**·**N**·**T**· ·

You may not need to do any of items 1 through 7. But, if you do, be sure you get started on them right away because they take the longest to accomplish.

What Areas Should I Fix Up?

The idea, of course, is to give your home a great look. You want "sexy" curb appeal. But you also want to have the rest of the property look good as well. Go through your property and check it out. Find out what looks bad, what looks okay, and what must be fixed for safety reasons. (You also may want to use the checklist at the end of this chapter.)

Generally speaking, here's what I suggest you do to make your house most appealing to buyers:

1. Fix Any Health and Safety Problems

This is obligatory because, first, you don't want anyone hurt because of something you could have or should have corrected. Second, you don't want the financial liability should someone be injured even after you sell the property. Therefore, check for any health and safety related problems.

•H•I•N•T •

You may want to employ the services of a home inspector here to help you determine what, if anything, is wrong.

Health and safety problems to correct:

- Fix any leaks in gas/oil furnace or heaters.
- Correct bad electrical wiring or connections.
- Repair cracks or breaks in the flooring.
- Replace broken glass doors or windows.
- Fix or replace faulty appliances.
- Fill or correct holes or trip areas in yard.
- Install smoke and carbon monoxide detectors as required by state law.
- Install earthquake/hurricane retrofits and safety measures as required by state law.
- Correct any other area of the property that poses a health or safety hazard.

2. Do All the Cosmetic Work to the Front of the Home

It usually doesn't cost much to make a good first impression with potential buyers. Indeed, good first impressions are often made by simple cosmetic changes. Remember the old Hollywood sets? What appeared to be an entire city was actually made up of a series of two-dimensional flats. What appeared to be buildings actually had no sides, back, or top. But when we watched the movie, the place looked authentic. It made a strong, believable impression.

·**H**·**I**·**N**·**T** ·

Never do safety work yourself; always have it done by a professional. If the next owner has a problem and is injured, you could be held liable for work you personally do.

It's the same thing for your house. Make sure you do your front cosmetic work. It's not expensive and it will make a big difference in terms of getting you a quicker sale and a better price.

Here's a list of what you can do to the front of your home that won't cost a great deal, but will make a big difference:

- Mow or replant the front lawn, water it, fertilize it until it looks terrific. Pull out any weeds. Rake or add gravel to paths.
- Plant colorful flowers near the entrance. Clean the driveway and any cement paths. If the entrance walk is broken or damaged, pull it out and replace it with inexpensive stepping stones. Make the front an eye-catcher.
- Wash and thoroughly clean the front driveway if it's cement or resurface it if it's tar. The first thing a buyer usually sees when pulling up to a home is the condition of the driveway.
- Repaint the front of your house. Use a good paint and a separate trim paint. Do an especially good job on the front door; even better, replace the front door with one of those elegant hardwood doors with beveled glass insets. If you're handy, you can do this on a weekend.

- Paint the inside entry of your home as well as the living room, dining room, and kitchen. Be sure not to use any garish color. This is another weekend's work.

You should be able to accomplish all of the above within a month at most and at a cost of under $500, if you do the work yourself (and don't buy the new front door). As a result, your house should make that great first impression.

3. Consider Whether to Do Any System Work

By system work I mean electrical, air-conditioning, plumbing, sewer, roof, or structural. If your evaluation of the property showed that work was needed in this area, it's time to sit down and make some serious decisions.

With the exception of roofing, virtually any work you do to the home's systems will not show. A buyer walking through won't know that you've ripped out all the old and leaking galvanized pipes and replaced them with new copper at a cost of $7,000. You won't get an extra $7,000 added to the purchase price—chances are you won't get 10 cents!

Nevertheless, should you spend the money?

That depends on how bad the problem is. If you've got old galvanized water pipes that leak in every room and the leaks are discoloring the paint on the walls and ceilings as well as warping the floor (don't laugh, I once owned a fixer-upper that had just this problem!), then you probably have to bite the bullet and get them replaced with copper piping. No, you probably won't get any additional money out when you sell, but if you don't do the work, you may not be able to sell at all.

On the other hand, perhaps you've got only one or two pipes with minor leaks. These can easily be repaired, at least temporarily, by a good plumber. (If you're handy, you can do it yourself with clamps found in most hardware stores.)

Now, you can cosmetically cover over any stains from previous leaks and sell "as is." This means you inform the potential buyers that there is a problem with the water pipes. They have leaked in the past and those leaks have been staunched. But they, or new leaks, could occur anytime in the future. You're not fixing it and the buyer has to take on the responsibility.

•**H**•**I**•**N**•**T**•••••••••••••••••••••••

By fully disclosing the problem to the buyer, you help lessen your liability for problems that could occur in the future.

If the buyers protest that they don't want to buy the house with potentially leaking pipes, you can bring in estimates for what it will cost to have the problem fixed (which you conveniently obtained earlier) and then offer to reduce the price by half the amount (or what is more enticing to most buyers, apply the amount to the buyer's nonrecurring closing costs, which means the buyer needs to come up with less cash to make the deal). Most buyers are more than happy to go along with such an offer, and it ends up costing you half of what you otherwise would have spent if you had fixed the problem yourself.

This applies even more when it comes to the roof. As homes get older, roofs deteriorate. While some types of tile roofs may last indefinitely, wood, tar, fiberglass, and other roofing materials wear out with time. Typically many roofs need to be replaced within about 20 to 25 years, although prior to this simple repairs will often suffice.

A new roof can cost anywhere from $5,000 to $15,000 or more. In other words, it's a big-ticket item. Should you go ahead and bite the bullet and have the work done?

My advice is to not have the roof fixed, although you may want to do minor repair work to ensure it doesn't leak and damage the inside of the property. There's an additional reason here: The new buyers may not like the color or the materials of the roof you choose. Indeed, you could actually lose a sale by putting the wrong roof on the house.

It's much better to indicate to the buyer that the roof is old, but that it's sound and doesn't leak. If the buyers want to replace it, it's up to them.

In most cases, the buyers will counter with an offer that asks you to replace the roof. After negotiation what usually happens is that, once again, you give them an allowance toward nonrecurring closing costs that they can use toward replacing the roof or for any other purpose. Usually, this will save you a considerable amount of money over going out and replacing the roof on your own.

4. Don't Do Unnecessary Remodeling or Add-Ons

Sometimes it's necessary to remodel just to get the market price for your home. For example, your kitchen may be outdated and may keep your home from selling. To get market price, or even a bit more, you put in a modern kitchen.

·**H**·**I**·**N**·**T**· ·

One of the few areas of the home where you can usually get out at least dollar for dollar spent is in the kitchen—but only if you don't overspend for the area. Put a $20,000 kitchen in homes that usually sell for $130,000 and you've wasted a lot of money. Put it into homes that sell for $400,000 and you may not have spent enough!

Or, every home on the block is 2,000 square feet. But yours is only 1,750; the other 250 feet is in an unfinished room. In order to get the full price, you may need to finish out that room. There may be good reasons why your home needs to have remodeling work done or why an addition must be put on just to get a decent sales price (and a quick sale).

On the other hand, many people remodel or add on because they just like the concept. They think they'll be making their house much more appealing. And they will, only it's unlikely they'll ever recoup the money they spent.

For example, let's say you decide to add oak bookshelves to a full wall of your living room for $4,000. But, you say to yourself, think of what I'll get when I sell. You imagine those shelves will turn the house into a must-buy proposition.

Unfortunately, that's not likely.

Chances are that your new bookshelves, attractive as they may be, won't get you a quicker sale or a higher price. In fact, while you'll be spending time, money, and effort, chances are you'll be getting nothing in return, except perhaps some satisfaction at seeing the work done.

Worst of all, when a buyer comes in and "oohs and ahhs" about your new bookshelves, that person is secretly saying to himself or herself, "What an idiot that seller is to have wasted all that money on bookshelves! Of course, I'll enjoy them, but why should I pay a dime more for them?"

This is even more the case when it comes to adding on rooms. Nothing costs more to do than to add additional space. A new room can easily cost $25,000 or more, far more than if it were added during the construction period. But, unless your home is much too tiny to resell for a good price, chances are you'll never recoup the entire $25,000.

I know of a family that nearly doubled the living area of their home during the brief three years they lived there. They added a second floor, enlarged the kitchen and family room and, in general, made their home into a palace. Unfortunately, that palace turned into a white elephant when it came time to sell because it was twice the size of any of the surrounding homes in the neighborhood. No one was willing to give them anywhere near the cost of the additions. They had to take an enormous loss on resale.

All of which is to say, unless you have to do it to get a sale, don't remodel and don't add on. In most cases you won't get your money out.

5. Don't Spend a Lot of Money or Time on Back or Side Yards

Your backyard may be a weed-strewn wasteland. You can't stand looking at it and you fear that potential buyers will be turned off by it.

So, you haul in sand and topsoil, lay cement for a deck, build an overhang, plant shrubs and flowers, and put in a small pond with a couple of fish. In short, you transform that desert in the back into a scenic park. Now, any buyer is going to be knocked over backward upon seeing your yard and rush to buy the property for a higher price, right?

Probably not. While most buyers love a great backyard, they won't pay ten cents more for it. It won't compel them to buy any quicker, either. They'll look at the front yard and the house and the first impression it gave and, if that's good, then they'll think about the backyard and add it in as a free bonus.

All that time, money, and effort spent on the backyard gets you a passing nod, but it doesn't make your house that much more salable. Much better to simply hire a neighborhood kid to come and mow the weeds down and turn over the soil. If it still looks bad, throw some grass seeds on it and water it until a lawn comes up. At least it will be green.

Don't waste money making your backyard into a work of art. Ninety percent of homebuyers aren't backyard lovers.

Are There Any Specific Hints on Fixing Up the Home?

Here are four hints that, when done properly, will make a great difference in adding sales appeal.

1. Get a New Front Door and Door Handle

The first thing a buyer physically touches on your house is usually your door handle. (Don't knock the tactile first impression—in many ways it's just as important as the visual impression.) Thus, the quality of your front door, and in particular the door handle, is vitally important.

Earlier I suggested you give the front door a good coat of paint. However, if you have the time, money, and inclination, I suggest you replace the front door and door handle.

A new solid wood front door with a glass insert costs around $500 and up. Add a few hundred more for installation. Yes, it's a lot of money, but it can make an enormous difference.

2. Use the Best Paint and Use Neutral Colors

After you've painted the front of the house and the entry rooms and fixed up the front door, I suggest you continue to paint the rest of the house. The next rooms to paint would be the kitchen, the guest bathroom, and the master bedroom, and then all the other rooms.

Paint them from floor to ceiling with a neutral color. It's important that the color not be strong like deep blue or green. Many people are offended by stronger colors. You could run into a buyer who loves a specific color. But for each one of those buyers, chances are you'll come across 50 others who hate it. You have to play the odds and go with the most neutral colors.

Also, buy the best quality paint, particularly if you're going to do the work yourself. The better the quality of paint, the better its "hide," or its ability to cover over and conceal the previous coat. If you use a top-quality paint, you can get by with two coats, or if you're very lucky, only one. Use a lesser-quality paint and you could spend the rest of your life painting and repainting the rooms of your home.

If your house has one of those acoustic-tile ceilings, popular in some parts of the country a few decades ago, do you paint it or remove it? Be careful here. Many of these older acoustical ceilings used asbestos as an ingredient. If you don't touch it, it may not be a problem; removing it could release dust into the air and become a real health hazard. Leave removal of acoustical ceilings to the experts. To paint it, you would usually cover it first with a sealing coat of shellac and then paint it with your normal paint.

3. Put In New Carpeting

When you first walk into a house or an office, your eyes tend to drift downward. We all tend to look at the floor. What do we see? Is your flooring bright, clean, and new looking? Or, is it dirty, worn, and frayed? The latter will make a negative impression on a buyer.

Perhaps the single biggest improvement you can make in a home is to replace the wall-to-wall carpeting. Brand-new inexpensive carpeting looks almost as good as brand-new expensive carpeting, and it looks a whole lot better than old carpeting, even if it's been cleaned.

Carpet prices, especially for good-looking, low-cost carpets, have actually come down in recent years. Further, you can often get real bargains on carpeting from carpet brokers (people who wholesale carpeting to landlords and others who buy in large quantities). Find a broker by checking with real estate professionals in your area, particularly those who handle residential property management. They are always replacing carpeting in homes, and most know several brokers who give them better deals. Most carpet brokers will be just as happy to deal with you as with anyone else.

For a 1,500-square-foot house, it might cost you between $1,500 and $2,000 to install a good grade of nice-looking carpeting. But be careful about color. The rule is that the carpeting always tends to look lighter when installed than it does when you look at a sample. When you're buying to live in the house, therefore, most people select darker carpeting. It doesn't show the dirt as much and it requires less cleaning. On the other hand, when you're installing carpet to sell a home, the rule is buy lighter carpeting. I have installed nearly white carpeting in homes I was preparing to sell. I wouldn't think of living in the house myself because I'd have to take off my shoes before walking on it for fear of tracking in dirt that would show. But it makes the house look fabulous for showing.

On the other hand, if you're pressed for money, at the least call in a professional carpet and floor cleaning service and have them do your house. Don't try to save money and do it yourself. Professional services can make even an old, worn-out carpet look better. They can make a floor shine. And in most cases they can do it for a couple of hundred dollars. The steam injector that you rent from the local super-market may only pump dirt from one part of the carpet to another.

4. Move a Third of Your Furniture to Storage

Most buyers want spacious homes. You probably did when you bought your last home.

Yet, over time as we live in our homes, we make them "comfy," usu-ally by adding furniture and a host of knickknacks. Unfortunately, too much furniture and odds and ends make our home look cluttered. When a buyer walks in, he or she may feel momentarily claustrophobic from the small amount of open space available.

·H·I·N·T ·

If you've had your home interior created by an interior de-signer, you may be reluctant to move anything out, and with good reason. Your home may already offer an excellent presentation.

The solution here is to remember that less is more. Be very strict and remove every piece of furniture you don't absolutely need. Make the living room spartan with just a couch or two, a chair, and a lamp. The dining room might just have a table, chairs, dish cabinet, and little else. And so on throughout the house.

When the place looks too empty to you, too thinned out, too foreign, it will probably look great to buyers. Remember, buyers are visualizing how their furniture will look in your home. It's important to give them the impression that their furniture will fit.

Where does the extra furniture go? In a pinch you can store it in the garage. Unfortunately, that means the garage will be cluttered and buy-ers like to see that they'll be able to put their own things (like a couple of cars) in there.

A better answer is to rent a small storage area and keep the extra furniture there. This can be quite inexpensive and, because you're going to need to box up the stuff for your move anyhow, it can save you time at the other end of the deal.

Another alternative is relatives or even friends. They might be willing to let you use a portion of their garage for short-term storage.

In any event, get rid of the overstuffed feeling and make your house a lean, mean, selling machine.

What Shouldn't I Do?

Here are five important things to not do, or at least to seriously evaluate before doing them:

1. Don't add a pool, spa, or deck. It costs a lot of money and you probably won't get much of a return. Even adding a lawn and shrubs to a back or side yard can be a waste of effort. Just stick with plain grass.
2. Don't add on to your house, unless your place is too small to command a good price, and only then if you won't be making the house bigger than its neighbors.
3. Don't remodel, unless you've got an outdated or worn-out kitchen or bath. Chances are you won't recoup the money you spent.
4. Don't fix the roof. Just be sure the leaks are patched. You can probably do better negotiating a compromise settlement with the new buyers than going ahead and spending the money yourself. Besides, potential new buyers might not like the roof you choose.
5. Don't fix major systems unless they are so bad off that they won't work. Remember, money you spend on items that don't show (such as furnaces, water heaters, air-conditioning, electricity, plumbing systems, and so on) aren't likely to be appreciated by buyers. In fact, they probably won't give you any money or credit for the big bucks you spend.

Get Started at Once

As you can see, there's a great deal to be done to fix up the typical resale, much more than most owners realize. To learn what you need to do, try the following checklist.

The Checklist: Fixing Up Your Home

❏   1. Are your front lawn, shrubs, and other greenery in great shape?

❏   2. Is your driveway and entrance walkway clean with no broken or cracked spots?

❏   3. Has the front of your home been recently repainted?

❏   4. Does the front otherwise look sharp?

❏   5. Do you have a high-quality front door?

❏   6. If not, is the door you have freshly painted?

❏   7. Are all glass and screens in tip-top shape?

❏   8. Does the paint throughout the inside of your house look fresh and clean with no marks or spots on it?

❏   9. If you have acoustical ceilings, are they clean?

❏ 10. Do you have a modern kitchen?

❏ 11. Is your house about the same size as its neighbors?

❏ 12. Are all light fixtures clean, unscratched, and looking good?

❏ 13. Is your roof in good shape? Does it look it?

❏ 14. Are all the systems (plumbing, heating, air-conditioning, water, sewer, and electrical) in good shape?

❏ 15. Is your house structurally sound from foundation through walls through ceiling rafters?

❏ 16. Are your back and side yards free from holes, pits, and other obstacles?

❏ 17. Are all your appliances working and in good shape?

❏ 18. Is your home spotlessly clean?

❏ 19. Have you asked others (such as agents) if there's anything else you've overlooked that you should do?

❏ 20. Will you hold off listing or showing your home until you're completely finished with your fix-up?

Don't feel bad if you've got a lot of unchecked questions. At least now you know what work you've got to do.

6

Weeks One to Six: Finding an Agent and Listing Your House

You won't have any trouble in finding an agent to handle the sale of your home. All you have to do is mention to a couple of friends that you're interested in selling and almost miraculously, an agent or two will call. Or, put up a small sign in front of your house saying, "For Sale by Owner" and you'll be inundated with dozens of agents wanting to list your property.

However, you don't want just any agent. You want an agent who, in addition to working hard and being honest and capable, will also work with you in your property juggling act. In other words, you want an agent who will sell your old home, find you a new one, and discount the commission along the way. (After all, it's two sales, not one.)

How do you find such an agent? You conduct a search.

Time Frame

You want to have the right agent lined up as reasonably soon as possible, certainly by the time you're ready to list. As noted in Chapter 4, you'll meet many agents while looking for new homes. In this chapter, we'll discuss other sources for finding good agents. The point, however, is that as soon as possible you want to line up an agent who will work with you, who will save you money on a double commission, and with whom you feel comfortable.

61

Further, you'll want to list your house. I've arbitrarily picked six weeks after you begin your juggling act as the time to list. But actually, it's as soon as you have your home ready to show. If you're only working on the house on weekends and there's a lot to do, it could be much longer, indeed many months. Or, if your house only needs some sprucing up, it could actually be just a few weeks.

In any event, you want to get your home listed as soon as possible. Selling it is, after all, half the work of the buy-sell equation.

How Do I Recognize an Agent Who Will Work with Me?

You'll want to interview agents, much as you would interview anyone else you were hiring. You'll want to make sure they are compatible with you. You don't want an agent you feel is too pushy or too laid back. You want someone who can get the job done, find a new home for you, and sell the old one. And, of course, you want an agent who will work with you by being willing to discount the commission for a double buy-sell.

This is a tricky subject with agents. Why would any agent discount the commission? Some agents won't even discuss discounting their commission, but many good agents are well aware that a seller-buyer such as yourself is a gold mine. You offer the potential of two commissions instead of one. Such agents are often willing to spread some of the wealth around in order to make sure they get both deals. Which is to say, they realize that it is reasonable to cut the commission on selling your existing home (where they act as a seller's agent) as well as on the purchase of your new home (where they act as a buyer's agent). After all, they make two deals and two commissions. That should be worth something.

How Much Can You Really Save?

We can all work the basic figures. Let's say the house you're selling goes for $200,000 and the one you're buying will cost $250,000. That's a round-trip of $450,000. Assuming a 6 percent commission, that amounts to a hefty $27,000 that goes to the agent(s). It seems easy to demand that the agent fork over a portion of it, say a third or more, which is $9,000. Wouldn't that be a nice savings?

However, these figures assume that the agent with whom you're dealing both finds a buyer for your old house and has the new house listed and, consequently, doesn't have to split the commission with another agent. And it also assumes the agent runs his or her own office and doesn't have to further split the commission with a broker. In the real world, all of the above assumptions are unlikely. Let's take them one at a time.

What's the Agent's Commission?

Let's assume you list your home at a 6 percent commission. On a $200,000 sale, that's $12,000.

•**H**•**I**•**N**•**T**• • • • • • • • • • • • • • • • • •

The commission rate is always arbitrary. It's what you and the agent decide on. It could just as well be 5 or 7 percent. Of course, some agents will refuse to work for less than an amount they feel is minimum. Indeed, you could be cutting your own throat by demanding a lower commission because it could induce agents to show properties other than yours that have higher commissions. (It would be unethical, but it does happen.)

If the agent with whom you listed finds the buyer for your property, the commission he or she will receive will indeed be the full $12,000. However, in the real world that's most unlikely. Better than 90 percent of sales are to buyers brought in by other agents. In other words, there will be two agents involved in just selling your property, yours and the buyer's. And they usually split the commission. Therefore, your agent's share is likely to be half of the selling commission, or $6,000.

Further, unless you're dealing directly with the broker in a small office, your agent will have to share that $6,000 commission with the office for which he or she works. The split with the office varies enormously. For an average agent, it's typically 50-50—the office takes half the commission, leaving your agent with just $3,000 (on the sale only of your home).

For a "good producer" (a strong agent), the split is usually much better, say as high as 80 to 90 percent. (However, in such cases your agent will usually have to foot his or her own bills for everything from phone calls, to copying, to advertising.) Your agent could get as much as $5,000 or more of the commission, before business expenses.

In other words, your agent is likely to get somewhere between a low of $3,000 to $5,000 (if the buyer is brought in by another agent) to as much as the full $12,000 (if your agent finds the buyer and operates his or her own office) out of just the sale of your property. How much of this is the agent likely to fork over to you because of the fact that you're offering a double deal?

What's Your Share?

Again, it's all a matter of negotiation. Some agents won't deal at all; others will be happy to. You simply have to find an agent who is amicable to dealing with you.

The agents with whom I've worked usually offer a sliding scale. If they find the buyer for your property and operate their own office, they might offer you as much as 30 percent or more of the commission. On just the sale of the home, for a $12,000 commission, that comes to a hefty $3,600, or more.

On the other hand, if they have to split with another agent and then split again with the broker, they might offer you far less, say only $500 or a $1,000. Nevertheless, even that is money you would otherwise simply never see.

What about the Commission on the Purchase?

Then, of course, there's the commission on the purchase of your next home. The same rules apply here: The commission your agent gets will vary depending on whether he or she is the listing agent and gets the full commission (very unlikely) and how much of a split must be given to his or her office. The percentages should be roughly the same, although the numbers will be different depending on your purchase price. Here again, you could save a low of only a few hundred dollars to a high of many thousands.

How Do You Negotiate the Discount?

Some people are too shy to ask for a discount from an agent, and most agents will discourage you from asking, saying that their commissions are firm, that they work hard for what they accomplish, and that they are entitled to the entire commission.

That's mostly true, although in a hot market where properties sell within a week or two after being listed, often for full price or more, that's hard to visualize.

On the other hand, you're bringing something special to the bargaining table—two deals instead of one. You could just as easily go to a totally different agent when you buy. So staying with the same agent for both the sale and the purchase is, reasonably speaking, worth something. And you can point that out in just the way I've done here.

A good agent will agree. Two commissions are better than one, even if there has to be a discount. And once you and the agent agree that there should be a discount, it simply becomes a matter of how much. The agent will probably spell out the commission split, much as I've done here, and indicate what he or she is likely to get. From there it's a matter of what you want to ask for and what the agent is willing to concede.

If an agent is adamant about not discounting a commission, I wouldn't insist on it. I would instead simply look for another agent. If you've signed with an agent you've pressured to take a lesser commission, he or she may feel cheated and do less to facilitate the sale of your house.

•⬤·⬤·⬤·⬤ ·

In your state it may very well be illegal for an agent to pay you, an unlicensed individual, a commission, in other words, to receive it and then "kick it back" to you. However, there's no reason an agent can't ask for less, in other words, charge you less. Be careful about how the wording is handled.

When Do You Get Your Discount?

You don't get it before the agent does. In real estate, commissions are paid only when the deal actually closes. In terms of the sale of your existing house, that's when you sign the deed and it's recorded in favor of the buyer. In terms of your next property, it's when your mortgage gets funded and title changes to your name. Unless both deals close simultaneously, the discount will be given at two different times, or more likely at the conclusion of the second deal.

What If You Move out of the Area?

It's important to understand that thus far we've been assuming that you move from one area to another within a local geographical area and that the agent you use services both areas. However, if you move to a different city, or a another state, or even a distant part of your state, you won't be able to (indeed you shouldn't) use the same agent for the sale of your existing home and the purchase of your next one.

The reason is that all real estate is local. That means that agents, over many years, get to know a particular small area—a city, a county or, in very large metropolitan areas, sometimes only a borough or neighborhood. But they know it very well. They know the price histories of property, the different types of homes, the schools, the crime statistics, business and job opportunities, and so forth. And their knowledge, in pricing and finding buyers for your existing home, as well as directing you to a suitable new home, is a large part of what you're paying a commission for.

However, when you move out of the area, you lose this expertise that the local agent offers. Indeed, many states recognize this fact and consider it unethical practice for an agent to try to work with a prospect at a distance from their locale.

Thus, if you move far away you'll need to work with two agents, your local agent where you used to live and a new local agent where you're moving to. But how do you save on a commission using two different agents?

It's still possible to get a discount, but it's more difficult. Many large real estate companies have offices across the state. Some big national franchise companies offer offices in virtually every state and community. When you work with an agent in one office, he or she can recommend you to an agent for the same company in a distant office.

However, most national companies do not have a policy of discounting for such referrals. Again, you can ask; I have seen discounts given in some cases. After all, you still offer the same advantage to the agents, two deals instead of one. But expect the discount to be significantly smaller, if at all.

Even if you deal with an independent agent, you can still negotiate a discount. Most local agents will contact another agent at a distant town on your behalf. If you subsequently buy through that distant agent, your original local agent may get a portion of the commission, sometimes 1 percent or more. And you may, thus, be able to negotiate a discount with your local agent and the distant one.

How Realistic Are Agent Discounts?

Discounts are a part of doing business for many agents. More than 40 years ago, my father was a real estate agent who had a successful business in California's Santa Clara Valley. He sold many properties. On some he received full commission; on others, he gave a discount. The difference? Some people asked and insisted; others didn't.

If the agent feels that the only way to make two deals is to give a discount, chances are he or she will negotiate. Remember, some agents will give discounts even on a single deal!

·**H**·**I**·**N**·**T** ·····················

When dealing with an agent who works for a national franchise, you probably will have to discuss any discounting with the broker. The agent himself or herself may simply not have the power to do this. Also, as noted earlier, discounting commissions for some is anathema; they won't even broach the subject, let alone discuss it.

How Do You Find a Good Agent?

Thus far we've been discussing an agent who will discount for a volume deal. However, you want more in an agent than just a discount. You want an agent who has the following attributes:

- Honesty
- Ability to get along well with people
- Current knowledge of the local housing market
- A knack for numbers
- Good judge of character
- Assertive, when necessary

The agent you get can make an enormous difference in getting your existing house sold as well as finding the right new home for you. With a good agent, the pursuit of a buyer for your existing home and location of your new home will be pleasant, negotiation will be handled with dignity, and chances are you'll be very pleased with the deals you finally get. On the other hand, with a not-so-good agent, every step of the way can be difficult, an agonizing problem where you're never sure you're getting the best service or deal, in short, where you feel you could've done a whole lot better.

Can You Get a Recommendation?

Probably the best way to get a good agent is through a recommendation. A friend or relative may have bought or sold a house recently and had a good experience. They're probably thrilled to tell you about their agent. Call that agent up and interview him or her. Ask how active he or she is (how many recent listings and sales he or she has). Get a list of properties he or she has sold over the past six months and the names and phone numbers of the buyers or sellers represented. Then call those people and see what they say. Are they satisfied as well? Are you satisfied with the agent? Do you feel comfortable with them? If so, you've probably got a winner.

Should You Try Just Walking into an Agent's Office?

You can always just walk into any real estate office and ask to see an agent. Like walking into an auto dealer's showroom, you'll immediately be introduced to the next agent who's "up," who's on duty to receive walk-in prospects. (Agents are assigned "floor duty" or time they spend in the office answering calls on ads and responding to prospects who drop in. In a larger office, there's a list and you get the next person on the list.)

Getting the next "up" agent is not necessarily a good thing. The newer agents are usually the ones who want floor time as it helps them get prospects. Often the more experienced agents have enough referrals to keep them busy. That doesn't mean they don't want a new client—every client is a potential sale and commission. It's just that you're not likely to get that better agent by just walking in.

Far better to walk in and ask to see the broker. (Each office is run by a broker.) Talk to the broker awhile and, if you are impressed with his or her qualities, ask if he or she will be your agent. After all, the broker is, presumably, the most experienced person in the office. Sometimes the broker will take time with you; other times, he or she won't have time to handle individual clients, but instead will leave that to other agents.

If the broker is not available to work with you, ask for the agent who's had the most sales and listings over the last year. You want someone who is actively, successfully working in the business. Then check that agent out by calling references, as we have discussed earlier.

What Are Other Ways to Find Agents?

As part of your house search, you'll undoubtedly tour many open houses. You'll quickly discover that the agent on duty there is trying to pick you up as a client. (The actual purposes of holding an open house are, in general, first to find buyers for the agent and second to give the appearance of doing something for the seller. Studies have repeatedly shown that a buyer who walks into an open house rarely buys that particular property.)

Talk to the agents at open houses. You may find one or two with whom you quickly strike up a rapport. Find out how active they are. And then check them out.

Of course, as a last resort you can always use the yellow pages, or call on an advertisement in the paper, or check the bulletin boards at grocery stores (or computer bulletin boards), or look for For Sale signs (which often list the selling agent), and then call the name of the agent who comes up most often.

Some people are inclined to use agents from national franchises. However, once again when you walk in, you're likely to get the first "up" agent available.

Don't worry, you won't have trouble finding an agent. As soon as you start looking, chances are, a great many will find you!

Questions You Should Ask Every Agent You Interview

We've already discussed getting referrals and checking them out. But here is a short series of questions to ask agents and what to make of their responses:

1. How many listings do you currently have?
Some agents do very well by listing properties. Unfortunately, they rarely sell the properties they list. They let other agents do that. These "listers" have simply learned how to get people to put their homes up for sale. You probably would not want this agent to work with you.

When you ask about current listings, you want the agent to be able to say that he or she has a number of them, perhaps as many as half a dozen. But if the agent has dozens and dozens of listings, then perhaps you've got a lister, someone who doesn't have the time or inclination to service all of these listings.

2. How many sales have you had in the past six months?
Some agents make their livings selling the property others have listed. Frequently they are sellers only, having few to no listings of their own. They tend to be assertive, sometimes even aggressive. If you don't buy with them the first or perhaps second time out, they dump you and move on to another client. One such agent I knew would qualify his prospects by telling them he had very high standards and expected them to live up to those standards, which included buying one of five homes he would show them. He said he picked the homes to show very carefully and qualified his buyers very carefully as well. If they didn't purchase, then they were at fault and he would have to move on. Of course, the lucky clients were the ones who didn't buy and saw this agent move on.

You want an active agent who has sold a number of properties; one a month would be excellent. Beware of the agent who's selling one a week—you could be high-pressured into making a deal you don't want.

3. Do you work part-time or full-time?   Many agents
have retired from other professions and see selling real estate as a way
to supplement their incomes. They work a few days a week and when
a deal comes their way, they're grateful for it. There's no rule in real
estate that you have to work full-time, although good offices demand
it of their sales forces.

The trouble is that the part-timer doesn't make a full commitment to
the business. This translates into the fact that the part-timers generally
don't get to be very good at selling, negotiating, pricing, or anything
else in the business. They're not on top of the market and seldom can
service their clients as well as a full-timer.

You don't want a part-timer to list your property or to help you find
a new one. You'd be wasting your valuable time.

If the agent hedges on the answer to the part- or full-time question,
ask how many actual hours a week he or she spends selling. (Full-time
agents put in 50-hour weeks.) Ask if they work mornings, evenings,
and all weekend long—full-time agents do.

What Is an Agent?

We've been using the term *agent* right along for six chapters in this
book as though everyone understood it. Certainly we all know the general meaning. However, it is helpful to understand the relationships
between the various people involved in real estate. Often the terms
agent, broker, REALTOR®, and others can be confusing. It can be a real
handicap for you if you're trying to find the most experienced person
in an office, yet don't know the proper terminology.

Agent.   Anyone licensed to sell real estate.

Salesperson.   The entry-level position licensed to sell real
estate. Usually in order to become a salesperson, you must not only
pass an exhaustive test on the legal, ethical, and practical aspects of
selling, but get a broker to sponsor you as well. Then, you must work

in the broker's office for a number of years (usually two) until you gain sufficient experience to become a broker yourself.

Broker.   A licensed person who has qualifying experience and has passed a more extensive qualifying exam. Only a broker can open and maintain a real estate office. One broker, however, can work for another. If the person with whom you're dealing tells you he or she is a "broker," you know you're talking with someone who is one level above a salesperson.

REALTOR.®   This is a broker who is also a member of the National Association of REALTORS® (NAR), a trade organization. The NAR offers seminars and programs that allow brokers to increase their knowledge in fields such as exchanging (trades), leasing (rentals), and business opportunities (commercial real estate). Usually a REALTOR® will quickly let you know if he or she has an additional designation awarded because of having taken additional training. Agents also belong to state and local real estate associations and boards, which are associated with the NAR.

REALTOR-ASSOCIATE.®   A salesperson who is a member of the NAR.

Licensed agent.   Any legitimate real estate agent. In all states, agents are regulated and licensed by state departments of real estate. These state departments establish rules and administer testing. They can hold an agent responsible for performing an unacceptable action and can discipline the agent by restricting or taking away his or her license.

Some states have recovery funds that allow you to receive compensation for an agent who has harmed you in a transaction. Of course, you can always sue the agent yourself if you feel you've been harmed. Most reliable agents carry heavy errors-and-omissions insurance just for this reason. (Of course, most reliable agents rarely, if ever, get sued.)

How Can You Work Better with Your Agent?

Finding a good agent is the first step. Once you've done that, you must help the agent help you. This means that you must determine how much you'll ask for your existing home and how much you can afford to pay for your next home. A good agent can help you immensely in this, not by pressuring you, but by providing information on past sales to help you make an educated decision.

It's important that you not be coy with your agent. Be as up front as possible. Tell the agent your expectations for the sale of your old house and the purchase of your new one. If the agents says you're being unrealistic, ask him or her to explain how. A good agent will take you around to current homes for sale (whether you're in your buyer or seller mode) to help educate you about what's out there. The agent wants you to know as much as possible, so you can act with knowledge.

At some point, you'll need to tell your agent something about your finances. While this may not be critical when selling, it is absolutely essential when buying as you'll undoubtedly need to qualify for a new mortgage in order to get your next home.

You basically need to let your agent know how big a loan you can swing and how much you can afford to put down. If you don't feel comfortable sharing this information with your agent, then perhaps you need to get a different one.

Should You Let Your Agent Coach You?

When you get offers on your existing home, you're going to wonder if you should accept, or if you should counter for more money. A good, trusted agent can give you solid advice here.

Similarly, when you find your next home, you'll wonder how much should you offer? Again, a good agent can be a great coach here.

Whose Side Is the Agent On?

This brings up the issue of who the agent is working for. Don't be misled into thinking that if you pay the commission, the agent is working for you. Technically speaking, who pays the commission has nothing to do with who the agent works for. Rather, it is up to the agent to decide and disclose this information.

You want an agent who works exclusively for you. That means that when you're selling, it's a seller's agent and when you're buying, it's a buyer's agent, even if it's the same person! Your agent should give you a written fiduciary statement declaring who he or she is representing.

The reason is simple. A seller's agent helps the seller get the highest price from the buyer. A buyer's agent helps the buyer get the lowest price from the seller. They are bound to do this both legally and ethically. That's why you want your agent to be a seller's agent when you sell and a buyer's agent when you buy.

·H·I·N·T ·

There's no conflict here if one person satisfies both functions for you. This agent would simply declare that he or she works for you in all circumstances.

Perhaps an example will help. This is the classic example used in all real estate classes. If a buyer tells a seller's agent that he will offer $100,000, but is willing to go to $110,000, that agent is required to tell the seller that even though the buyer is making an offer of $100,000, he'll go $10,000 higher.

On the other hand, if a seller tells a buyer's agent that although she's asking $100,000 for the property, she'd actually be willing to accept $90,000, that agent is required to tell the buyer that the property can be had for $90,000. That's why it's important to make sure your agent represents you in all cases.

Sometimes agents will assume a dual role, representing both buyer and seller. While this is legitimate in most states, I personally don't think it's realistic. Just as no slave can serve two masters, no agent can serve two adversarial clients.

How Will I Know If I Make a Bad Choice of an Agent?

You'll know soon enough.

You'll find that no one comes by to see the home you're trying to sell. (A good agent will arrange for other agents to "caravan" or tour the home and will constantly be "talking up" the property to keep other agents interested.) And after a couple of hunting expeditions, you'll find that the agent doesn't call to show you property you can buy.

Your relationship turns into one of, "Call me if you see something you want."

In short, you'll discover that instead of your agent working for you, he or she is sloughing off on the job. Your existing house isn't getting sold and you aren't finding a new one. In short, you feel that your agent has dumped you, so you want to dump him or her.

•**H**•**I**•**N**•**T**• •

Loyalty deserves loyalty. If your agent is loyal to you, be loyal to her or him. As we've seen, it will save you money and it will keep that person working hard for you. One thing agents seldom forget or forgive is a client who they spend countless hours on, and who then buys from someone else.

If you're unhappy with the performance of your listing agent, call the agent, explain how you feel and tell the agent you want the listing back. Talk to the broker as well as the salesperson. Often a few simple calls can get you out of the listing, particularly in a slow market. After all, real estate is a business where reputation is very important. Agents don't want someone running them down because they didn't give back what was probably considered a dead listing.

Occasionally, you'll get an agent who won't give you your listing back. (When you sign a listing, you make a binding commitment to the agent, one you usually can't back out of.) The agent may feel ornery, or that he or she eventually can find a buyer. You can complain to the agent's broker, to the local board of REALTORS®, even to the state licensing department. But unless the agent has actually done something wrong, there's little you can do. Your best bet may be simply to wait until the listing expires and then try it again with someone else. (This is a good reason never to give a listing for more than 90 days.)

What about Selling It Myself?

Here, instead of getting a discount on the commission, you want to save the entire sales commission. Can you? Should you?

Yes you can. However, keep in mind that you'll have to do all of those things an agent does and you'll be at a big disadvantage. The agent belongs to the Multiple Listing Service, an organization of other agents working with hundreds, often thousands, of prospective buyers, many of whom may be interested in your property. Indeed, one of the things you gain by working with an agent is their network.

If you're considering selling FSBO, my book, *The For Sale by Owner Kit,* 3rd Edition (Chicago: Dearborn, 1998) will show you how.

I always suggest that to avoid feeling you could have saved a bundle of money if only you'd tried to sell FSBO, you do try it, at least for awhile. Pick a short period of time: a few weeks, a month, two months. Give it your best FSBO shot. If you're successful, you've saved yourself a pile of money. If not, give up and list. At least you won't regret that you never tried and you won't have wasted a great deal of time, either.

What Should I Look For When I List?

The listing is intended to be a legally binding contract. Therefore, you should read it thoroughly before you sign, as with all such contracts. It's also not a bad idea to have an attorney check it over. Remember, once you sign, you may be committed to what's in the document.

There are a couple of critical areas you will want to check out in the listing discussed next.

How Long Is the Listing For?

The listing should have specific start and termination dates. My suggestion is that you never give a listing for more than 90 days. If you don't sell within this time frame and you like your agent, you can always relist with him or her. On the other hand, if you don't like your agent's work, after three months you're out and can go elsewhere.

Beware of agents who try to pressure you for longer listings, particularly in a down market. They may point out that it's taking six months to sell a home. That may be, and you can say that if you're satisfied with the agent's performance over the first three months, you'll extend the listing for another three. But there's no need for a longer commitment on your part. Keep it short and you'll have more control over your agent.

How Much Is the Commission?

This is normally spelled out as a percentage. It could be any percent. There is no set or "legal" rate. The most common commission rates nationwide are between 5 and 7 percent. Discount brokers will often list between 3 and 4 percent.

What Kind of a Listing Is It?

Real estate listings differ in the degree to which you are committed to pay a commission. The least commitment on your part comes from an open listing. Here you simply agree that you'll pay the agent a commission if he or she brings in a buyer. However, if you sell the property or if some other agent brings in a buyer, you're not committed to paying a commission to the agent who didn't bring in the buyer.

On the other end of the scale is the exclusive-right-to-sell listing. Here you agree to pay a commission to the agent with whom you sign no matter who brings in the buyer, even if you find the buyer yourself!

In between is the exclusive listing. Here, you agree to pay a commission to one agent only, no matter what other agents find a buyer. However, if you find a buyer yourself, you aren't committed to pay any commission.

Many people new to the field are apt to think that the obvious best choice is the open listing. Indeed, I recently even saw two authors plugging a real estate book on television telling the viewers that because of the lesser commitment on the part of the seller, this was the way to go. Nothing could be further from the truth. The best listing is the exclusive right-to-sell listing, the one that most commits you to pay a commission no matter who finds the buyer.

·**H**·**I**·**N**·**T**· ·

Watch out for a net listing. Here the agent agrees to accept as commission anything above a specific price. For example, the net to you may be $100,000. Anything over this is the agent's. The problem is that you make it too easy for the agent to take advantage of you. The agent could sell the property for $150,000 and pocket $50,000! I wouldn't sign a net listing. It's too difficult to control and too easy to abuse. Indeed, in some states, net listings are considered unethical and illegal.

Why? The reason has to do with performance. You're interested in getting your home sold. You want the agent not only to put up a sign, but to advertise in local papers, send out mailers, talk up your house to brokers, in short, to spend a great deal of effort getting it sold.

But no sane person would do this if you can undercut him or her either by selling directly to the buyer yourself, or by giving the commission to another agent. In other words, if you want the agent to perform for you, you must demonstrate that you are committed to paying for that performance.

If you give an agent an open listing, that agent will likely throw it into the bottom desk drawer and not think of it again unless a buyer comes along and demands to purchase your property. If you give an agent an exclusive listing, the agent may think about it, but will always worry that you'll try to make a deal with any buyer who comes by from the sign in front or elsewhere. The agent simply won't be willing to spend energy, time, or money on such an iffy proposition.

But, if you give an agent an exclusive-right-to-sell listing, that agent knows there's a commission at the end of the rainbow and, if he or she is any good at the business, will work hard to get it.

Don't be misled or confused. You want performance, the agent wants commitment. It's a fair trade-off.

The Checklist: Finding an Agent and Listing Your Home

●●●

❏   1. Are you working toward finding an agent and listing within six weeks?

❏   2. Are you currently interviewing agents?

❏   3. Are you asking them for a discount on the buy-sell round-trip?

❏   4. Are you asking others to recommend an agent?

❏   5. Have you asked an agent you're considering, "How many listings do you currently have?"

❏   6. Have you asked an agent you're considering, "How many sales have you had in the past six months?"

❏   7. Have you asked an agent you're considering, "Do you work part time or full time?"

❏   8. Do you understand the difference between the terms *agent, salesperson,* and *broker?*

❏   9. Do you understand that a seller's agent does not hold a fiduciary relationship to you as a buyer?

❏ 10. Are you aware that once you sign a listing, it could be very hard to get out of early?

❏ 11. Are you going to try to sell by owner (FSBO)?

❏ 12. Is there a definite termination date in the listing you'll sign?

❏ 13. Have you negotiated a reasonable commission rate?

❏ 14. Is this an exclusive-right-to-sell listing?

❏ 15. Do you understand why an exclusive-right-to-sell listing is probably the best type of listing for you?

If you find you're hesitating over certain questions, just remember that if you want to get a better deal on the buy-sell round-trip, you must find a good agent who will work with you, and you must get that house of yours on the market as soon as it's ready to show.

7

As Soon as Possible: Making an Offer on Your Next Home

Ideally, on the day that your old home sells, you'll find and purchase a new home. The escrows for both houses will move along simultaneously and will close on the same day—a perfect double transaction.

In the real world, things rarely work out so neatly. More likely if you wait to buy your new home until you sell your old one, you'll have months between transactions that can negatively affect your lifestyle, your finances, and even your health.

If you're following the time line suggested in Chapter 2, you began looking for your next home the second day you committed to the buy-sell juggling act. Now you've found the home of your dreams. But you haven't even had a nibble on the old property. Maybe you've been fixing it up and haven't even listed it! Are you out of luck? Do you simply grit your teeth, turn away, and hope that this perfect house will still be there when your old house finally sells (perhaps months down the road)?

You want to buy your next home as quickly as you can, but I'm sure some readers are wondering if purchasing a new home before selling the old one isn't putting the cart before the horse. After all, where will you get the money for the down payment? How can you handle two mortgage payments? What if you can't sell your old home?

These and others are legitimate questions. Indeed, the cleanest and safest way to purchase any home is with cash down and a clean slate behind, no old payments or old house to worry about. That, in fact, is probably how you did it with the first home you purchased.

But now you have to handle things differently. You've got an existing house and your situation is different. Now you have to handle things differently. You've got to coordinate the move, compete in the marketplace, and deal with the sale of an existing home.

In fact, there are many ways of tying up that new house before you sell the old. Some of these techniques may work for you and may ensure that you can have your cake and eat it, too. That's what we'll discover in this chapter.

What If I Find My New Home before I Sell or Even List My Old Home?

What you're dealing with here is a high level of uncertainty. Your old home could sell tomorrow—or next year. You really can't be sure. What you want to do is tie up the new property with a minimum of financial risk to yourself.

There are at least two ways to do this: the option and the contingency clause.

What Is an Option to Buy?

If you've played the stock or commodities markets, you've undoubtedly heard of an option. Options also are used in real estate, although they are far less common and less well known.

Any seller can give you an option to purchase his or her property. What you are offering, basically, is to pay a set price for the property within a fixed period. In a well-drawn option, the terms of the purchase are spelled out just as they would be in a sales agreement. The time is also indicated, such as 90 days or six months.

In essence, you can purchase the property at your option any time within the time frame. The seller has committed to sell and technically can't back out of the transaction. Remember, it's at your option, not the seller's.

You must pay a fee for this privilege, The fee can be any amount, but for options of under six months, it's typically a thousand dollars more or less, depending on the value of the property. On a more expensive property, the option price could be significantly higher.

The option money is given to the seller and it's his or hers, regardless of whether you exercise your option. This is an important concept to grasp. Once you hand it over, the money is spent. It's gone.

However, many options provide that if you decide to go ahead with the purchase, the option money will be considered part of the down payment. This isn't necessary and if it isn't written into the option, won't apply. In that case the option money would be over and above the down payment (and the purchase price).

Why Would You Want an Option from a Seller?

It's simple; it ties up the property. The seller can't sell to someone else while you hold the option. The seller can, indeed must, sell only to you.

·**H**·**I**·**N**·**T**· ·

Try to get the option recorded; if it isn't, the sellers could sell the home to someone else in the interim and if they did, your only recourse might be to sue them in court. If recorded, it forms a cloud on the title and the sellers can't give clear title until it is removed. However, recording may require that all parties sign and have their signatures notarized.

Further, you aren't at great risk. If you decide not to exercise the option, you're only out the option money. You don't have to worry about the sellers coming back and suing you for specific performance (demanding that you complete the purchase) or damages (because you failed to purchase). It's clean and neat. If you decide to exercise the option, the property is yours. If you decide not to, presumably because you didn't ever sell your old house, you're out only the option money.

In addition, if you couldn't buy at the end of the option period, but the home had gone up in value, you could potentially sell your option to another buyer for a profit!

Why Would the Seller Give Me an Option?

Options are commonly used in commercial real estate transactions. Here they are for big money (typically the buyer puts up $10,000 or more for the option) and allow a prospective buyer to tie up a property while arranging for financing, investigating a market, or planning an overall financial investment strategy. Sellers like them because they generate cash without the seller having to really do anything. If the property doesn't sell, the sellers get the money from the option. Even better if a deal can be made, because then the property's sold.

The same reasoning applies to sellers of homes. First, it's an opportunity to make contact with a legitimate buyer (one who's willing to put up some money). Second, if the property doesn't eventually sell, the seller still gets the option money. And third, there's always the chance the property will sell.

The biggest problem you'll face with an option is explaining to a seller what it is and its benefits. Most people understand a sales agreement, but few if any have ever seen or heard of a real estate option. Nevertheless, once the benefits are explained, a seller *may* wish to go along with it.

Will Market Conditions Affect the Option?

I emphasize *may* because a lot depends on the housing market at the time. How agreeable a seller will be to an option offer usually is related directly to housing market activity.

Let's say the housing market is strong with well-priced properties typically selling within 30 days or less of being listed and you want a six-month option. If the sellers are pretty confident that by doing nothing, they can land a cash buyer in a month, why would they want to give you an option? To their way of thinking, the most they can lose by turning you down is 30 days in finding a buyer and the option money you give. On the other hand, if they accept and you wait the full six months to exercise your option (if you ever do), they've lost at least five months during which their property could have been sold.

In short, you'll find the option a difficult tool to use in a hot market. The only way to make it work better is either to increase the amount of the option money or decrease the time you want. For example, asking for just a 30- or 60-day option and putting up $1,500 might sway some sellers.

It's a different story if the market is weak. Here, sellers are sitting on their properties for months at time. Six months may seem like a short time to sell a home in such a market and getting cash in hand as well as a potential buyer by means of an option may seem like a great alternative. In a weak market you probably will find sellers falling all over themselves to accept your option.

·**H**·**I**·**N**·**T**· ·

Be aware that many sellers not only must sell, but also must move. Therefore, what they are actually looking for is a "lease-option." They want the buyer to rent the property during the option period. That gets them out and starts money coming in with which they can make mortgage and other monthly payments. You, however, are offering only a straight option. Therefore, you need a seller who doesn't need to move out quickly.

Most markets are somewhere between strong and weak. It may take 90 to 120 days to sell a typical property, although some may sell sooner and others later. Here, you'll likely find some sellers who will accept an option and others who won't. You'll simply have to give it a try and see what the sellers say.

How Do I Negotiate an Option?

You'll need to negotiate with the sellers. There are basically three negotiating points:

1. Will the sellers consider an option?
2. How much money will they want?
3. How long a term will they give?

Obviously, with sellers who will consider an option, you want to give the smallest amount of money for the longest term. They will want the opposite, the most amount of money for the shortest term.

The terms that are eventually agreed on will result from the market conditions (as explained earlier), how eager the sellers are to go along, and how eager your are to get the property.

I suggest you negotiate the option in two steps. Present it, then negotiate terms.

1. Present the idea of an option and explain it thoroughly.   Remember, for most sellers this is a strange, new thing. It may even be new to their real estate agent. You'll want to take it very slowly explaining how it works and the advantages to them. You may even want to secure a copy of an option (we'll discuss how later) and bring it along to show.

2. Next, only after the sellers understand and are seriously considering the option, negotiate the terms.
For this, you need to be on your best bargaining behavior. This usually means being forceful but polite, repeating the advantages to the sellers, and using the other techniques of successful negotiation. For more on this, read my book *Tips & Traps When Negotiating Real Estate* (New York: McGraw-Hill, 1997).

Will the Listing Agent Go Along?

Another issue is whether the property listing agent (assuming the sellers are not trying to sell it themselves) will go along with an option.

Remember, the agent is looking forward to a sale and a big commission. With an option, the commission is greatly reduced. Further, the agent may need to release the sellers from the sales terms of the listing before they can execute an option.

This is not to say that the agent won't be compensated if the sellers take an option. Some listing agreements call for the agent to receive as much as half of the option money in such cases. In others, the agent receives only a small percentage of the option, roughly equal to a rental commission. In yet others, there is a set fee if the sellers decide to option the property.

You may have to make it worthwhile to the agent (in addition to the sellers) to get him or her to agree to go along with an option. In a slow market, this isn't going to be a hard sell. In fact, the agent may be happy to get a couple hundred dollars for releasing the listing with the understanding that he or she will collect a full commission later on if you exercise the option; or that he or she will get the listing back if you don't.

In a hot market, the agent may not want to go along, anticipating a coming quick sale. Indeed, the agent may work hard to convince the sellers to hold out for a straight sale, instead of giving you an option. You will find it difficult to succeed in getting an option if the agent is against you.

Where Do I Get an Option Form?

Any good real estate attorney can draw one up for you for a nominal fee. Any good real estate agent can arrange for one to be drawn up for you, sometimes for nothing.

What you want to avoid is picking up a ready-to-fill-out option form from your local office supply store. These tend to be generic forms that are designed to fit many situations; rarely are they specific enough to deal with a unique case. In other words, the forms need to be fleshed out by a good attorney who can add the correct wording as well as make them appropriate for your state laws.

Can I Buy Property Contingent on the Sale of My Old Home?

Another way to purchase a home before your sell your existing house is to do it with a sale contingency. Using this gambit, you offer the sellers a standard sales agreement specifying how much cash you'll put down, the mortgage you'll get, and any other terms you want.

In addition, you insert a clause that says the purchase of the home is "subject to" the sale of your existing property. This is a contingent sale. There's no deal at all until your old property sells.

It's important to understand exactly how this works. All your purchase terms are spelled out, including the amount of your down payment, your deposit, the term, interest rate, and type of mortgage you're getting, as well as your demand for an inspection and any other demands you may have. And the statement that the sale is contingent "subject to" the sale of your existing home is included.

Negotiating the Sale Contingency

Negotiating the purchase is done in the normal fashion, with the sellers probably demanding an increase in the sales price or changes in the terms. Undoubtedly, they also will demand that you remove the contingent sale clause, knowing that it weakens your offer. As long as you refuse to remove it, and they eventually go along with this, you've got a contingent sale.

·H·I·N·T ·

Attempting to buy a home without the cash for the down payment and without a contingency clause that lets you wait until you cash out the equity of your existing home, opens you up to great peril. If the seller accepts and you're later unable to complete the transaction, you could lose your deposit. Plus, although unlikely, the seller could sue you for specific performance (demanding that you complete the transaction) or for damages.

If the sellers finally agree to the purchase agreement, along with your contingent offer, it essentially means that the new house is yours, when and if you sell your existing home. If there's no sale of your existing home, then there's no purchase and you're entitled to get your deposit back and walk away from the deal.

Why Would I Want a Contingent Sale?

The reason is obvious—it protects you. You lock up the purchase of your next home while giving you time to sell your existing home. Further, if for any reason your existing home fails to sell, you are under no obligation to buy the new home.

The big advantage of the contingent sale, that it protects you so well, is also, unfortunately, its biggest drawback. After all, why would sellers want to give you so much protection?

Why Would Sellers Sign a Contingent Sale?

Generally speaking in a strong market, a seller's agent will argue against signing a contingent sale. The agent will point out that it ties up the sellers' property while in no way guaranteeing them that the property ever will be sold. Indeed, it means that the sellers now have two sales to worry about—the sale of their own property and yours as well!

In short, in a strong market, sellers are very unlikely to be amenable to a contingent sale. They almost certainly will consider it, and then just as certainly reject it or modify it. If they modify it, you have to be very careful about what their modifications are.

How Will Sellers Modify the Contingent Sale?

Sellers who are willing to accept a sale contingency may want to modify the terms of your "subject to" clause to favor them. There are several ways they can do this. The first is to agree to it in general, but insist that it include a *first-refusal* clause.

A first-refusal clause is still a contingency and still allows you to back out anytime until your house sells. However, it adds a new element. Now the sellers can continue to look for and receive offers from other buyers. If another buyer comes in with an offer to purchase, then you have right of first refusal. Typically you have 48 or 72 hours to remove your contingent sale clause. If you don't, your deal is null and void and the sellers can feel free to go on to sell to the second buyer.

Let's be sure we understand how this works. In a conventional sale, once the deal is signed, you've tied up the property and are usually awaiting only clear title and a new mortgage to close the deal.

With a contingent sale clause, you've tied up the property and are awaiting the sale of your existing home before proceeding with the purchase.

With a first-refusal clause, you've tied up the property only until another buyer comes along. When another legitimate buyer shows up with an acceptable offer and a deposit, you have a few hours to remove your contingency, or lose the deal.

Adding the first-refusal clause allows the sellers to have their cake and eat it to. It allows them to sign with you, while giving them the opportunity to look for other buyers. Should another legitimate buyer show up, they can demand you buy almost immediately, or they can sell to that other buyer.

Should you agree to modifying the sale contingency with a time limit? Only if you have no other choice. It may come down to a situation where the only way the sellers will go along with a sale contingency is with a first-refusal clause. Then you have to decide just how badly you want the property and whether you want to go through the agony of waiting, hoping your house will sell before another buyer for the new home comes along.

How Do the Sellers Find Another Buyer if the Property Is Sold to You?

Typically along with a first-refusal clause, the sellers also will insist on a *right-to-show* clause. This specifies that even though they have agreed to your contingent purchase, they have the right to continue showing the property as if it had never been sold. Indeed, most often a "sold" sign will not be posted on the property.

Will other buyers actually make offers in such a situation? Some won't, believing instead it's a waste of time. They'll worry that they'll make their offers, and then just when they think they've got the property, in you'll come and steal the deal away from them.

Others, however, reasoning that you won't be able to remove your contingency clause because you haven't sold your house (if you had, you already would have removed it), will make an offer. Thus, while the sellers probably won't get as many offers this way, some determined buyers will still make offers.

Can the Sellers Set a Time Limit?

Another way sellers can modify a contingent sales clause is to set a time limit on it. Yes, they'll go along with you and they agree to your contingent clause, but they'll give you only 30 days or 60 days or some other specific amount of time within which to remove the contingency. If you haven't sold your house during that period, the deal is void and they're free to sell to someone else.

In some ways, a time limit is better for you than a first-refusal clause. With the first-refusal clause, you never know day to day whether you've bought a home or not. With a time limit clause, you know that it's yours until a set date and you've got that long to come up with a buyer for your property.

How Difficult Are Contingent Sales Clauses to Negotiate?

We've seen several ways in which sellers might modify a contingent sales clause to make it more favorable to them. On the other hand, they might simply refuse it out of hand—or accept it as is. A lot will depend on their own motivations and, once again, on market conditions.

In a very strong market, you'll have great difficulty getting sellers to accept a contingent sale clause, even with modifications. They'll simply feel that it's a waste of time. Why should they waste time on you when they are likely to catch a cash buyer within just a few days or weeks?

It's a different story if the market's weak. If the house has been sitting for four months and you're the first offer to come along, the sellers are very likely to take your offer seriously. Yes, they might attempt to modify it, but at the same time, they don't want to lose you. After all, a contingent buyer is far better than no buyer at all.

Who Do I Get to Write In the Various Clauses?

The proper answer is to have a real estate attorney do it. The wording is critical.

On the other hand, a great many real estate agents who have been in the business for a long time know how to do it as well as, if not better, than some attorneys. If you've got a competent agent, have him or her write it in for you.

Beware of doing it yourself. You might inadvertently add a few words that would allow the sellers to get out and be able to sell to someone else. Even worse, you might add something that ties you in such a way that you can't back out without losing your deposit.

In today's litigious society it's well worth the expense to spend a few extra bucks to get it done right. On the East Coast where they predominate, real estate attorneys typically charge only between $500 and $1,000 to handle an entire transaction. There's probably no better bargain in law today.

What If I'm Forced to Complete the Purchase before I Sell My Existing House?

It could happen. You could have a contingent sale with a time limit or with a first-refusal clause. Another buyer could come along or your time could run out. Now you've got to go through with the sale or lose the property. Or the sellers could refuse any kind of sale contingency at all, demanding instead a straight purchase on your part.

In short, you've got to put up or shut up. You've got to buy or back away from the deal.

My suggestion is to back away. Although Will Rogers remarked that the one thing about real estate was that they aren't making any more of it, the fact is that there are plenty of homes available on the market. The supply may dry up a bit in a strong market and get overly plentiful in a weak market, but homes there are. If the one you're trying to get doesn't work out, often the best course is to simply let it go. Another, perhaps even better, deal will come along.

But, you say, this is your one and only dream house, the perfect place for you. You can't let it go. You must get it. How?!

The old maxim that where there's a will, there's a way applies here. If you insist on going forward in spite of the risks, there are a number of ways you can buy your next home without first selling your existing one.

Can I Get My Cash Out?

There are usually two problems with attempting to purchase another home before you've sold your own: coming up with the down payment and qualifying for the new loan. In terms of the down payment, the problem arises from the fact that the equity you want to use to purchase the next home is still tied up in the old home. Because you haven't sold, you don't have the cash (unless you've got a big bank account, which is an entirely different matter).

The question then becomes, how do you get that equity out of your old house into your new home? Assuming you're a reasonably good credit risk, it's not difficult.

1. Try for a bridge loan.   As the name suggests, a bridge loan spans the gap between your old home and the new, which is why it also sometimes is called a "gap" loan. In essence, it cashes your equity out of the old home and puts it into a down payment for the new.

Most banks and some mortgage brokers offer bridge loans. To get one, simply describe to the lender what you're looking for. Typically the loans are for a relatively short period, usually six months or so.

Here's how they work. Let's say you have $50,000 in equity in your current home. The lender may loan you $40,000 for six months or a year, payable at interest only, provided you use all of that money toward the down payment of your next home. (Normally, money for a down payment may not be borrowed, but in the case of a bridge loan, exceptions can be made, especially if there's also seller financing, which will be described shortly.) When you sell your existing home, the bridge loan is repaid.

The problem with bridge loans is that they tend to be costly. The lender has the risk that you won't be able to sell your existing home and, thus, won't be able to repay the bridge loan. That could force the lender to foreclose. Because of this risk, you'll end up paying a higher interest rate on your bridge loan than on a straight first mortgage.

2. Get a home equity loan. These are available from banks and are about as easy to get as credit cards. All you have to do is apply, have enough equity in your existing home to warrant the loan, and have enough income to make the monthly payments, which are usually interest only. Interest on these loans is typically only about 2 percent higher than for standard real estate loans.

·H·I·N·T ·

As noted, many lenders won't allow borrowed money to be used for a down payment. Hence, you must get the home equity loan far enough in advance of the purchase that it can't be construed as having been borrowed specifically for that reason. Usually three months to six months is a reasonable time frame.

A home equity loan can be used to fix up your property, pay for a college education, or just about anything else, including a down payment on another house. They are, however, usually limited in the amount you can get. Typically you can't get more than 80 percent of the value of your property, less existing financing. (The combined value of all loans cannot exceed 80 percent.) That means that if you owe 65 percent in an existing first mortgage, the home equity loan couldn't be for more than 15 percent of the home's value.

3. Consider seller financing.   A decade ago, seller financing was the rule. Today, it's seldom done, which is a shame because, if properly handled, seller financing can benefit all parties to a transaction.

Here the seller becomes the lender and gives you enough money (actually a loan in the transaction) to complete the purchase. For example, let's say you're buying a home for $100,000 and need $20,000 down. The seller gives you a short-term loan for $20,000. Just as in the bridge loan, you agree to pay it back as soon as your existing home sells, and you agree to pay the seller a healthy interest rate.

Again, the problem may arise that, with this much financing, the institutional lender may hesitate in granting a first mortgage on the new property. If that's the case, have the seller put the second mortgage not on the new property, but on your existing one and give you credit (not a loan) as part of the purchase transaction. This way you'll have no extra financing on the property you're purchasing.

The second mortgage on your old home can have an "alienation clause" specifying that the loan to the seller of your new one must be paid off as soon as you sell the property. It also can have a due date, say six months in advance, which will usually help placate a seller's worries about ever getting paid.

Having the seller help with the financing is a great way to go, because the seller is likely to be motivated to help you out in order to get a sale. Further, you don't have to go through all the hassle of qualifying for mortgages. Most sellers only require that you submit a reasonably good credit report.

Further, sometimes sellers are eager to help with the entire financing. This is particularly the case with retired couples who are looking for strong income sources. If they cash out of the sale, they may be planning to stick their profit in a savings account or certificates of deposit. If you offer them a sound investment with a higher interest rate than they can get at a bank, they may jump at it.

Can I Make Two Sets of Monthly Payments?

If you own two homes, chances are you're going to have to make two sets of payments. That means not only two monthly mortgage payments (assuming you only have one loan apiece on the properties), but two sets of taxes, insurance payments, homeowners fees, utilities, and so on. In short, you could easily double or more the amount you're paying currently.

Impossible, you may argue. I can't possibly do that!

Actually, you very likely can, if it's for a short time. If it's only for a few months, then what you need to do is to calculate the total amount of money you'll need for the monthly payments, subtract what you can afford monthly, and then see about the rest. You might take it from savings, or borrow it from relatives, or you might borrow it from the bank. I've known several people who have handled a short-term double payment by borrowing money on their credit cards. No, it's not the cheapest way to go, but if you're getting a bargain on the overall deal, it might just be worth it.

•❿•❶•❽•❶ •

Be careful. You can never know for sure how long a transaction will take. If it hinges on the sale of your existing home, be prepared for it to take longer than anticipated. You might have trouble finding a buyer. The buyer you find might back out of the deal. Anything could happen. A good rule of thumb is to prepare for things to take at least twice as long as anticipated.

Be aware that you'll have to disclose that you have two sets of payments to an institutional lender on your new home. These higher monthly expenses could affect your ability to qualify for a new loan. On the other hand, you could move into the new home and rent out the old one, hopefully for the mortgage payments. The rental income will help offset the extra mortgage payment expenses. (Not totally, however; lenders normally won't allow rent to completely offset mortgage and other rental home payments because of the risk of vacancy.)

Should I Bite the Bullet and Own Two Homes?

Many people have done that. I have done it myself. Yes, that means two mortgage payments, two sets of utility bills, two yards to maintain, and on and on indefinitely. But if I really like the new home and if I'm determined to get out of the old one, I, and you, just might be willing to do it.

Again, once you move out of the old home, you probably can rent it out. If you've lived there for awhile, chances are appreciation on rentals has progressed to the point where you may be able to rent it out for enough money each month to cover your mortgage, tax, and insurance payments. Suddenly you're a landlord.

Of course, there are problems associated with renting out your existing home. We'll discuss some of these in Chapter 12.

What about Walking Away from the Deposit?

One high-risk strategy is to walk away from the deposit if you're unable to complete the purchase. Usually the most you're likely to lose is your deposit; however, if handled badly, you could end up the defendant in a lawsuit by the seller.

Here's how it works: You put up a deposit of as little as possible on a property in order to secure a deal, which is written with a very long escrow period, during which you hope to sell your own home. If you do sell, you go ahead and complete the new home transaction; if you don't, you attempt to extend the escrow and, failing that, lose your deposit. (I said it was "high-risk"!)

The danger here is not so much that you'll lose your deposit, which is presumably what you're willing to risk. It's that an angry seller will then sue you either for specific performance (an unlikely situation in which you are required to complete the transaction), or pay damages for failure to go through with the deal.

Any size deposit agreed to by both buyers and sellers will work, although sometimes sellers state that they don't want to be brought offers with a deposit of less than, for example, $10,000. I've never known an agent to not bring in an offer no matter what the deposit amount. There is nothing to say that you must offer a large deposit. I've bought $400,000 homes with only a $5,000 deposit, and the seller seemed happy to get that!

The way to protect yourself is to get the seller to sign a "liquidated damages" clause in the sales agreement. Today most sales agreements contain such a clause; however, it is not effective unless both buyers and sellers sign. You can refuse to go through with the transaction unless the sellers sign. Once they do, presumably, they've agreed to accept your deposit in lieu of suing for damages if you fail to follow through. Be aware, however, that this alone may not keep a determined and angry seller from pursuing you legally, although it will undoubtedly bolster your case.

Be aware that you're supposed to have access to the cash for the down payment when you make an offer. If it's tied up in equity in your old house, you're supposed to disclose that to the sellers. Being aware of this and failing to disclose it could be considered unethical conduct on the agent's part. Smart sellers will insert a clause in the sales agreement insisting that you provide proof of funds to complete the transaction within a few days after signing.

Sellers in a soft market are much more likely to accept a deal with a small deposit than when the market's hot. In a strong market, sellers may still accept the deal but write in a clause that within a relatively short time, say 14 days, you increase your deposit substantially. The seller understands that there really is no deal until you've removed the standard contingency clauses for disclosures and inspections. (If you're not sure what these are, see Chapter 8.) In other words, as long as you can back out at any time simply by refusing to accept the inspection or whatever defects, if any, the sellers disclose, it really doesn't make any difference how big a deposit you put up. It's only after you've signed off on the contingencies that the deal begins to solidify. And it's at that point that the sellers may insist on a bigger deposit. If so, you've tied up the property for a few weeks at best, unless you're willing to pump more money-at-risk into it.

A modern real estate transaction is really much different from one of only a few decades ago. Back then, the deal was made when you signed the purchase agreement. Today, the deal is really made only after all the contingencies have been removed. Indeed, one way to describe a modern real estate transaction is as an ongoing process of slowly tying up the buyers by removing contingencies, until finally a contract that can't be broken is made.

The Checklist: Making an Offer on Your Next Home

❏   1. Have you found a home you really want?

❏   2. Are you ready to make an offer, even if you haven't sold your old home?

❏   3. Do you understand how to use a real estate option?

❏   4. Can you give the seller reasons to accept your option?

❏   5. Can you give the listing agents reasons to go along with your options?

❏   6. Do you understand what a "contingent sale" clause is?

❏   7. Can you give the seller reasons to accept the contingent sale clause?

❏   8. Are you ready to accept or reject the seller's possible modifications to the contingent sale clause?

❏   9. Do you have a plan of action to follow if the sellers find another buyer before you've sold your existing home?

❏ 10. Are you willing to get expert help (a good agent or attorney) to aid in writing in the appropriate clauses?

❏ 11. Do you understand how a "bridge loan" works, and how to get one?

❏ 12. Have you considered a home equity loan to help with your down payment?

❏ 13. Will seller financing help you? Will seller financing help the seller?

❑ 14. Can you handle two monthly payments for a short time?

❑ 15. Are you willing to walk away from your deposit and risk being sued for damages?

Making an offer and buying your next home can work, as long as you understand the risks and take precautions.

Coordinating Two Escrows, Disclosures, and Inspections

Thus far we've been working with a time line dedicated to getting your old house sold and finding a new, acceptable home. But what happens after you've found a new home, and made a deal on it, and found a buyer for your old property? What do you concentrate on now that you've got two deals in the fire?

A New Time Line

Your goal now is to coordinate the timing of both the sale and purchase of two properties. If things have worked out fairly well for you, you will have two homes in escrow. (An escrow is normally used to handle the closing of a real estate transaction—an independent third party is given the deed, the cash, and all necessary materials and then, when everything is in order, records the deed and distributes the monies.) The ideal is for both of them to close at the same time. If they close simultaneously, you can accomplish the following:

- The equity in your old home is converted to cash and can be transferred to the new home as a down payment.
- You can move directly from your old home to your new one.
- You can avoid any double charges for interest, taxes, insurance, and other fees you would incur if you owned two homes simultaneously.

All of this hinges, of course, on both deals closing simultaneously, ideally on the same day. But, is this a realistic possibility?

Can I Really Close Two Escrows Simultaneously?

Yes, you certainly can. It's done all the time. However, for it to work, you'll need the cooperation of escrow officers, lenders, and the agents involved. And you'll have to stay on top of the situation to be sure that all the legwork involved in closing actually gets done by the deadlines.

It's important to understand that what we're talking about here are two distinct escrows. This is not "double escrowing," a real estate term that means buying a property and then reselling it, for a profit, to a second party while never actually owning it. Double escrowing is generally frowned upon because often one or more parties are unaware of what's happening. (Full disclosure is an ethical, and in many cases a legal, requirement.) Here, we are simply talking about escrows on two different properties, something much different.

If you are using the same agent both for selling your existing home as well as for buying your next one (as described in Chapter 6), you'll find the whole procedure goes much easier. If separate agents are involved, you may find some conflicts that tend to work against you. (One agent may want to close sooner than the other.)

Overall, if you plan it correctly and things go reasonably well, you should have few problems closing both deals simultaneously.

Creating a Time Line for Simultaneous Closings

A house's strength lies in its foundation. Build a solid foundation and you'll have a strong house. The same holds true with closing two escrows. Build the right conditions into both escrows and things should work properly. Therefore, the key to success lies in what you put into the sale or purchase contracts.

Before You Sign the Sale or Purchase Contracts

The following key elements should be included to help "grease" the deals:

1. Be sure you leave enough time to close both deals. With one escrow, you can be fairly sure that a couple of things will go wrong, which will take time to correct. With two escrows, multiply the things that can go wrong by four, not two. In other words, you want to allow as long as possible for the escrows to close so that you can overcome unexpected difficulties. I would suggest escrows of at least 45 days on both properties.

·H·I·N·T· ·

I always operate on the premise that everything that possibly can go wrong will and that it will take twice as long as expected to fix it. Therefore, the rule is the more time allowed, the better.

The buyer of your existing house or the seller of your new one, however, may not want to go along with a long escrow. They may, reasonably enough, want to close their deals quickly, perhaps in 30 days. What do you do in this case?

One answer is simply to make the long escrow a condition of the sale or purchase. You won't go along with either deal unless the other parties agree to the extra time. The problem here is that one or the other (or both) of the other parties also may be adamant about a shorter escrow. They may be in the process of buying or selling other property and need a shorter escrow. Your choices may come down to either agreeing to less time or losing the deal.

One argument you may use to avoid the above dilemma is to point out to the other party that you only want a long escrow because you've got two deals in the fire. If things go well, then you'll agree to an earlier closing. If the other party is reasonable, he or she may agree to this. If not, you're no worse off than you were before you proposed it.

2. Be sure you leave yourself a way out.

Include an escape clause in the purchase contract. A typical one would be that the close of your new home purchase is contingent on the close of the sale of your old home. If you can't close on the old, you can get out of the purchase of the new.

This will considerably weaken the contract. However, it also will allow you to sleep better at night.

If the seller of your new home refuses to go along, you can always try it without such a clause. However, if you can't close on your old home, you could be in hot water, as discussed in Chapter 7.

3. Set the closing for both escrows on *the same date.*

This way, everything on both deals will be working toward the same goal. Typically many things in the escrow are left to the last minute. For example, the new loan you want to get (as well as the new loan the buyer of your old home wants), normally isn't funded until the very last minute. With both escrows scheduled to close simultaneously, everyone (including the lender) knows when this is. If one escrow is set to close before or after another, however, and later on you want to close them simultaneously, you could have difficulty in getting funding on both at the appropriate times.

4. Try to use the same escrow company.

There are two reasons here. The first has to do with funds. To close simultaneously, you'll need to transfer funds obtained from the sale of your old property to the down payment for your new property. The transfer of funds can be a sticking point if there are two separate escrows.

In the old days, it would take time to hand-carry a check from one escrow company to another. Plus, there would be time lost while the receiving escrow company waited for the check to clear (up to three days or more).

Today, electronic transfers make things easier. You can have funds transferred almost instantaneously. However, I have seen electronic transfers get screwed up. The sending bank delays making (or forgets to make) a timely transfer. Or the amount isn't exactly correct. Or the receiving bank can't find the funds for a couple of days.

All of these problems can be alleviated if the same escrow company handles both transactions. Transferring funds simply becomes a matter of moving them from one account to another in the same bank. Therefore, insisting on the same escrow company for both deals can facilitate fund transfers at the last critical moments.

·**H**·**I**·**N**·**T**· ·

You may not be able to use the same escrow for both your purchase and sale. The seller of the home you are buying, for example, may insist on a different escrow company. This may be the case when dealing with a national franchise firm, which will want to use a designated escrow. I've seen it happen, admittedly rarely, where the whole deal comes down to which escrow company to use. If you can't use the same escrow company for both deals, don't panic. Separate companies will work too, although probably not as well. It will just mean that you will have to be especially vigilant in tracking the close.

Another reason for using the same escrow company is the coordination of activities involved with the closing. You'll need to get and give disclosures and inspections, as well as secure financing and see that the other party secures financing and clear title. With one escrow company (and, presumably, one escrow officer), it's a lot easier to keep track of what's been done and what remains to be done. It's also easier to learn of a problem at an early stage when it can most easily be corrected.

5. Tie both deals together.   As noted earlier, an escape clause is always a good idea. It's also a good idea to have a clause inserted that links the two escrows. Something as simple as stating that both escrows are to be coordinated and are to close simultaneously puts everyone on notice that this is a double deal. It also may be an additional way out for you in the event things go wrong. If both escrows can't close simultaneously, then all parties may be entitled to simply leave the deal unscathed. This, however, is less sure than the escape clause noted earlier.

·H·I·N·T· ·

As with all clauses to a deal, you should have your attorney check over the clauses linking the escrows for efficacy and consequences.

Immediately after the Deals Are Signed

As noted earlier, disclosure is a big part of real estate transactions today. As of this writing, about 30 states require sellers' disclosures. With two deals you have two sets of disclosures to worry about.

1. Carefully read the disclosures.   The sellers of the home you are buying should give these to you. They should list any defects. (Look over the disclosure list given later in this chapter.)

If no defects are listed, it presumably means that there are none or that the sellers know of none. This is very important because if later on (after you're living in the house), some defect appears that the seller *should have known about,* but didn't disclose, you may have good grounds for going to court and securing damages. For example, suppose the sellers disclose that there are no problems with the roof, yet after the first rain you find multiple leaks coming into the house. Then, when you call the local roofer to fix the roof, that person says the company has been out half a dozen times to fix that same roof on your house and told the seller on each occasion that the roof would never stop leaking until it was replaced, you have every right to be angry with the seller and to take appropriate action.

When reading the disclosures, pay special attention to any area that's likely to require expensive repairs, such as the roof, the foundation, the structure, and the building systems (such as electrical, plumbing, wastewater, and so on).

In many states you have several days after receiving the disclosure to back out of the deal without penalty. (In California, for example, you have three days after the sellers give you the disclosures.) If something really bad turns up, you may want to exercise this right.

2. Prepare and give the buyers your disclosures.

Now the shoe is on the other foot. You need to give the buyers of your home disclosures about what's wrong with it. And, because of the fact that in many states the buyers can back out if they dislike something in the disclosures, it's important that you get these to them as soon as possible. Ideally you would have prepared them well in advance and have them ready to hand out as soon as (or even before) the deal is closed.

The question for most sellers is how much to disclose. It should be evident that what you don't disclose could later come back to bite you. On the other hand, what you do disclose could discourage the buyers from going through with the deal.

My suggestion is that you disclose everything. The more you disclose, the less your liability is likely to be. For example, if you disclose that your roof leaks and needs to be replaced and the buyers accept the house anyhow, they are going to have a hard time later on coming back and bellyaching about a bad roof. They knew before they bought (because of your disclosures) and they took it anyway.

What's most likely to happen if you disclose a bad roof (or any other defects) is that the buyers will come back and ask you to remedy it. They'll ask for a new roof, for example.

·**H**·**I**·**N**·**T** ·

Some sellers will order their own home inspection to find out if something hidden is wrong with the property. Once discovered, they can then fix it before the sale. Of course, the sellers should still disclose the problem, who fixed it, and how.

Now you can negotiate. You can say you're willing to pay half the price of a new roof or fix the old one. They may agree or may simply want money given back to them in escrow (that they can apply to the roof or to their closing costs, for example). In short, in most cases with a sincere buyer, something can be worked out.

The solution is to get the problem on the table up front. The worst thing you can do is to hide it (for example, by doing some temporary patching, plastering, painting, repairs). Nothing looks worse than a seller who not only fails to disclose a defect, but gets caught trying to conceal it.

·**H**·**I**·**N**·**T** ·

Be especially careful when it comes to health and safety issues, such as a leaking gas line. Innocent buyers could move in not knowing of the defect and be injured in a fire or explosion. I automatically correct any health and safety defects before sale to avoid this serious liability issue.

Figure 8.1 is a list of some of what you should include in your disclosure. This is a partial list taken from my book, *Seller Beware* (Chicago: Dearborn, 1998).

FIGURE 8.1 • Disclosure List

Environmental Disclosures

My property has the following environmental conditions:

❏ Asbestos (insulation, ceilings, fireproofing)

❏ Common walls, fences, or driveways

❏ Contaminated water supply (public)

❏ Contaminated water supply (well)

❏ Discoloration of vegetation

❏ Earthquake—property within fault or seismic hazard zones

❏ Earthquake—retrofitted

❏ Earthquake—weakness in structure

❏ Elevated radon levels (in neighborhood)

❏ Elevated radon levels (in or under house)

❏ Encroachments by neighboring properties

❏ Excessive noise (from dogs barking, neighborhood children)

❏ Excessive noise (from other sources _____)

❏ Excessive noise (from planes, trains, trucks, freeways)

❏ FEMA—property within flood hazard area

❏ Flooding (past or present)

❏ Flooding or poor drainage of neighboring properties

❏ Formaldehyde emitting materials

❏ Fuel storage tank(s) (above ground)

❏ Fuel storage tank(s) (underground)

❏ Lead-based paint on any surfaces (location)

❏ Near military training facilities (past or proposed)

❏ Near mines or gravel pits (past, current, or proposed)

FIGURE 8.1 • Disclosure List (Continued)

Environmental Disclosures (continued)

❏ Near pending real estate development that could affect value

❏ Near ravines where disposal may have occurred

❏ Near toxic dump site

❏ Near waste disposal site

❏ Pet feces or urine in flooring (location_____)

❏ Pet odors (location _____)

❏ Poor drainage (past or present)

❏ Rights of way or easements on property

❏ Sinkholes

❏ Traces of asphalt, concrete, metal in soil

❏ Traces of toxic elements in soil

❏ Urea-formaldehyde foam insulation

Electrical System Disclosures

My property has the following:

❏ 110-volt electrical system

❏ 220-volt electrical system

❏ 100-amp circuit breakers (main)

❏ Fuses (main)

❏ Ground wire to all electrical services

❏ Ground-fault interrupter circuits in kitchen, baths, and wet areas

❏ Grounded—electrical system to cold water pipes

❏ Cover plates on all outlets

❏ Any electrical not up to building code

FIGURE 8.1 • Disclosure List (Continued)

Plumbing System Disclosures

My property has the following:

❏ Contaminated well (on property)

❏ Copper piping

❏ Galvanized piping (age, leaking?)

❏ Leaks (location_____)

❏ Rapid change in water temperature (shower, sink, _____)

❏ Slow drainage

❏ Standing water (any location)

❏ Toilet cracks

❏ Water heater strapped according to building code

❏ Water pressure (high)

❏ Water pressure (low)

❏ Well water pump (date installed)

Heating and Air-Conditioning System Disclosures

My property has the following:

❏ Air-conditioning system leaks

❏ Clothes dryer adequately ventilated

❏ Ducting damaged or in need of repair

❏ Furnace heat exchanger damaged or in need of repair

❏ Furnace room adequately ventilated

❏ Temperature/relief valve on water heater

❏ Vents in place throughout

❏ Water heater adequately ventilated

FIGURE 8.1 • Disclosure List (Continued)

Structural Disclosures

My property has the following:

❑ Abandoned septic tank

❑ Building, cracking, or other problems with retaining walls

❑ Ceiling insulated (R-factor of insulation _____)

❑ Crawl space below ground level

❑ Chimney damaged or in need of any repair

❑ Damage or change from settling, slipping, sliding, grading, or from filled ground

❑ Downspouts empty away from building

❑ Floors insulated (R-factor of insulation _____)

❑ Gutters and downspouts in good/bad repair

❑ Roof leaks

❑ Roof repaired or replaced within past three years

❑ Room additions (with permit)

❑ Room additions (without permit)

❑ Screens on all windows in good repair

❑ Structural wood below ground level

❑ Vapor/moisture barrier

❑ Walls insulated (R-factor of insulation _____)

❑ Windows broken or cracked

FIGURE 8.1 • Disclosure List (Continued)

Ownership Disclosures

My property has the following:

❏ Assessments, bonds, or judgment liens against property

❏ Boundary disputes

❏ CC&R deed restrictions

❏ Common area(s) (location _____)

❏ Easement(s) (location _____)

❏ Homeowners association

❏ Lawsuits filed by or against the seller that may affect the property

❏ Lawsuits that may affect the homeowners association or any common areas

❏ Leases against property

❏ Notice of default filed against property

❏ Notices of abatement or citations

❏ Right of first refusal to another party

❏ Third-party claims against property

I have the following:

❏ Real estate license

❏ Contractor's license

❏ A person on the title who is not a U.S. citizen

Reports Disclosures

The following inspection reports were made during or before my ownership of the property.

FIGURE 8.1 • Disclosure List (Continued)

	Available?	Date of Report	Who Made Report
☐ Air-conditioning system	Y N	_____	_____
☐ City/county inspection	Y N	_____	_____
☐ Drainage	Y N	_____	_____
☐ Energy audit	Y N	_____	_____
☐ Geologic	Y N	_____	_____
☐ Heating system	Y N	_____	_____
☐ House inspection	Y N	_____	_____
☐ Pest control	Y N	_____	_____
☐ Roof	Y N	_____	_____
☐ Septic tank	Y N	_____	_____
☐ Soil	Y N	_____	_____
☐ Structural	Y N	_____	_____
☐ Toxics inspection	Y N	_____	_____
☐ Water system	Y N	_____	_____
☐ Well	Y N	_____	_____
☐ Other	Y N	_____	_____

Other Disclosures

I am aware of defects in the following:

Explanation

☐ Ceilings _____

☐ Doors _____

☐ Driveway _____

FIGURE 8.1 • Disclosure List (Continued)

Other Disclosures (Continued)

☐ Fences _____

☐ Floors _____

☐ Foundation _____

☐ Insulation _____

☐ Roof _____

☐ Sidewalk _____

☐ Slab(s) _____

☐ Walls _____

☐ Windows _____

☐ Other Areas _____

All work done on the property authorized by me was done by a licensed contractor and has a completed building permit on file except _____

In addition, the following matters could affect the desirability or the value of the property _____

_____

_____

The Day after the Deals Are Signed

Because you can't do everything at once, as soon as you've finished with the disclosures, probably the next day, you need to order an inspection of the property you are purchasing.

Today every wise buyer will insist on an inspection to check that all of the home's many systems are in good shape. If problems are discovered, you then can negotiate with the seller over how to handle them (as indicated above with disclosures), what should be done, and who should pay for it.

The buyers of your home will undoubtedly order an inspection of your property. You will need to order one for the home you are purchasing. In all cases it is customary for the buyers to pay for the inspection report. These days it usually costs between $250 to $350 for a residential property.

·**H**·**I**·**N**·**T**· · · · · · · · · · · · · · · · · · · ·

Keep in mind that as a seller, you want an inspection, too. Your should be concerned that the buyers could come back after a sale and claim there is a defect in the property that you didn't reveal. The buyers could sue for damages, even rescission of the sale. (*Rescission* means the seller would have to take back the property and refund the money.) However, if the buyers order their own inspection and it doesn't reveal anything, then you're on much firmer ground.

There are a number of concerns with inspections, both when you order one on the house you're buying and when the buyers order one on the house you're selling. These include the following:

1. Finding a good inspector. It's important to understand that home inspection is a relatively new field (under ten years old in most areas) and inspectors in almost all areas are not yet licensed. Therefore, you have to be doubly careful in selecting one.

Look for members of national trade associations. For example, many inspectors belong to ASHI (American Society of Home Inspectors). Others belong to NAHI (National Association of Home Inspectors). These are growing organizations and have qualifications for membership. In addition, ASHI provides standards of inspection that can be very helpful.

You can ask for recommendations. The broker with whom you're dealing should be able to recommend a home inspector. You can call your local building and safety department. Sometimes home inspectors are retired from local building departments. These are the people who regularly go out and inspect property for the city to be sure it meets code. They are well versed in what to look for in a home and have had extensive experience with people who sometimes try to cover stuff up. Also, these types of inspectors tend to be more candid than others.

For technical reports, consider structural, electrical, and even civil engineers. If you find the same name popping up over and over again after checking the sources we've discussed, you may have a winner. Interview the inspector, using the same interviewing techniques you used with the agents—get at least three referrals and call them to see how they liked the inspector's work.

2. Get the inspection report.   The document that says what the inspector finds is too often simply a printout generated by a computer "home inspection program." The inspector simply plugs in his or her data and then the computer generates the report. Too often these reports fail to draw any concrete conclusions that you as buyer will find useful. Therefore, I suggest you go along with the inspector of the home you are purchasing. Ask questions. You may find out a great deal more verbally than ever gets put in the report.

Similarly, go along with the inspector of your own home. As suggested, inspectors vary enormously in their abilities. They may see something innocuous and think it's terrible. For example, as a seller, I once went along with a buyer's inspector (and the buyer) and when we went into the subbasement, the inspector said, "Aha." He pointed to metal braces going from the support beams down to the foundation. "Obviously," the inspector said, "this house has had problems shifting on the foundation. That's very serious and could be very costly to correct." The buyer was shaken.

However, because I was there I was able to point out that the braces were actually retrofitting the previous owner had installed to protect the house in the event of an earthquake. Needless to say the inspector was red-faced and his derogatory comments never appeared in the written report. And the buyer was relieved. It only happened this way, however, because I took the time to go along.

Also, as a seller, when the buyer demands a clause in the purchase contract allowing for an inspection and time to approve it (which is acceptable), you should insist on receiving a copy of the written report. If you don't, only the buyer gets it. You may need that report later on if this buyer backs out of the deal and you need to show it to a subsequent buyer, or if much later on there's an issue of liability and disclosure.

3. What the report covers.   Inspection reports are by their nature, cursory. The inspector comes to the home and spends a couple of hours there. He or she can't look at and find everything. Further, many areas are inaccessible and can't be inspected. For example, if there's wall-to-wall carpeting, it's highly unlikely that you're going to peel it back to look at the floor underneath. (You may decide to peel back a corner in one room, but you're not going to take off all the carpeting.) In addition, some areas, such as parts of the attic, parts underneath the house, inside the walls, and elsewhere, simply are not accessible at all.

The written reports themselves will typically exclude any areas that are not accessible. They also typically will have all sorts of caveats protecting the inspector in case he or she overlooks something, or finds something that later turns out to be nothing.

In short, too often these written reports are highly superficial. Which is another reason to go along with the inspector. He or she is much more likely to give more helpful verbal comments than those bland comments that will likely later appear in the written report.

The Day after the Day after the Deals Are Signed

Again, you really need to do this as soon as possible, but you can't do everything at once. So as soon as you get time, the next thing on your agenda should be to let your lender know you've found a property (assuming you were preapproved or even if not).

The lender will order an appraisal, which should take no longer than a week to complete (but which might take longer if it's a hot market where there are many sales and appraisers can't get out quickly). The appraisal then has to be formally submitted to the lender who has to accept it, which can take more time. You'll have to pay for the appraisal, which typically will cost around $250 to $300 for a residential property.

The lender also will order (if it hasn't already as part of your preapproval) the three-bureau credit report discussed in Chapter 3 to be sure that your credit is sufficiently good to warrant the financing you're seeking.

Until the Escrows Close

You'll need to monitor both deals on at least a weekly basis (more often if there are problems). You'll want to see that everything is proceeding smoothly. The last thing you want is to wake up on the morning of the day the deals are to close only to discover that an intractable problem has surfaced, that will take many weeks to correct.

As a buyer you should track the following to be sure everything is proceeding apace:

Your credit approval. Is your credit report satisfactory? If not, what exactly are the problems and how can they be corrected? Once you find out, correct them. If they are not correctable, you may not be able to finance the purchase. (This is another good reason why preapproval is so important.)

The home appraisal. Has it been done? If so, did the property you're buying appraise for enough? If not, you might have to come up with more money, you may want to go with a different lender and a different appraiser, or you could submit comparables to show that the appraiser was in error and ask for a reappraisal, or renegotiate the price.

Your cash down payment. Do you need to cash in bonds, stocks, or other assets to get the cash for the purchase? If so, find out how long it takes and make arrangements to get this done in a timely fashion.

Repairs to the property.   If the inspection or disclosures revealed any problems that the sellers have agreed to correct, are they being done in a timely fashion? If not, contact the sellers and their agent and be sure to stay on top of this. Usually the purchase cannot close until all work mentioned in the purchase agreement (and subsequent addenda) has been completed.

As a seller you should track the following to be sure everything is proceeding apace:

Title clearance.   To sell you must normally give clear title. But there could be a "cloud" or obstruction recorded against your title. For example, an old judgment may never have been removed. Or there could be a problem with the name on the deed. The variety of problems that can crop up can be endless. Usually these can be cleared up, but it takes time. You should check with the title insurance company handling the sale of your home on a weekly basis to find out if anything untoward has appeared. Usually, but not always, the title company will call. But it's far better for you to stay on top of this.

Buyers' removal of contingencies.   Remember, it really isn't a deal until the buyers have removed all of their contingencies. This includes disclosures, inspections, and any other contingencies. Your agent should track this for you, but it won't hurt for you, as the seller, to keep track yourself.

·**H**·**I**·**N**·**T**· ·

Contingency removals are of two kinds—active and passive. In the active kind, the party has to give written approval. In the passive kind, failure to give written disapproval amounts to approval. Be sure you know what kind of removals are called for in your case and that they meet the deadlines set up by the sales agreement.

Repairs to the property.   As part of the sale of your existing home, you may have agreed to make certain repairs. Be sure these are on target to be done before the date designated for closing the deal. (Very often a termite report, required by almost all lenders, will reveal some damage. Be sure it is cleared up in a timely fashion.)

You need to track other areas, such as the moving of your furniture, the establishment of utilities in your new residence and their turn-off at your old, arrangements for storage (if necessary), and so on. (These are covered in detail in Chapter 12.)

The Day before the Closing

Just before escrow closes, it is common practice to have a "walk-through" of the property. The purpose here is to ascertain that the premises are in as good a condition as they were at the time the deal was made. With two deals, you have two walk-throughs to consider. (The walk-throughs must be written into the purchase and sales agreements, or else they won't be done.)

As a buyer, you will want to inspect the home you are buying carefully. It should be in relatively good shape. If the sellers have moved, expect to see minor dirt and scratch marks where their furniture was. But there should be no unexpected broken windows or screens, no holes in the walls, floor, or ceiling, or anything else that might be considered major damage. The property also should be fairly clean.

As a seller, you need to be sure that your property shows at least as well as it did when you signed the sales agreement. The yards and lawns should be well watered and trimmed, and the inside of the house should be neat and clean. You'll probably want to spend special attention cleaning the kitchen and bathrooms, which is where most buyers look for dirt.

If as a buyer you find a problem with the walk-through, you should immediately report it to your agent and the sellers and ask that it be corrected. You will probably want to hold up the closing until it's done.

On the other hand, if the buyers find a legitimate problem with a home you're selling, you will want to immediately correct that problem to be sure it doesn't hold up the sale.

The walk-through is sometimes used by buyers to try to wiggle out of a purchase they don't want, claiming that the property is damaged goods. This seldom works these days and could result in throwing the entire deal into litigation.

The Day the Deals Close

On the day the deals close there's the matter of the paperwork. There are all sorts of documents to sign and items to pay for. Closing is such a big and important function that we'll cover it separately in the next chapter.

The Checklist: Coordinating Two Escrows, Disclosures, and Inspections

• •

Before You Sign the Sales or Purchase Contract

❏   1. Have you left enough time to close both deals?

❏   2. Have you left yourself a way out?

❏   3. Have you set the closing for both escrows on the same date?

❏   4. Are you able to use the same escrow company?

❏   5. Have you tied both deals together?

Immediately after the Deals Are Signed

❏   6. Have you read the sellers' disclosures carefully?

❏   7. Have you carefully prepared and given the buyers your disclosures?

The Day after the Deals Are Signed

❏   8. Have you found a good inspector?

❏   9. Have you written in a clause ensuring you'll get a copy of the buyer's inspection report?

❏ 10. Do you understand the limitations of the written report and why you should go with the inspector during the inspection?

The Day after the Day after the Deals Are Signed

❏ 11. Have you contacted the lender about getting a mortgage and appraisal?

Until the Escrows Close

❏ 12. Are you tracking your credit approval?

❏ 13. Are you getting together the cash for your down payment?

❏ 14. Are you tracking any repairs to both properties?

❏ 15. Are you tracking title clearance for both properties?

❏ 16. Are you tracking your buyers' removal of contingencies?

The Day before the Closing

❏ 17. Is your property ready for the buyers' walk-through?

❏ 18. Are you ready to walk through the property you're buying?

.... **9** ...

Saving Money When Closing the Deals

To close the sale of your old home, you'll need to give the buyer clear title, which is usually evidenced by a policy of title insurance. To close the purchase of your next home, you'll also need title insurance to guarantee your ownership and to get financing. In addition, you'll need to have two escrows that will handle the closing of both deals. And you'll need to take care of a great number of fees that crop up when a real estate transaction takes place.

All of these cost money. In this chapter we'll look at the costs and see where and how to save money.

Can I Save Money on Title Insurance?

Who pays title insurance is usually a matter of custom for the area in which you live. For example, in some areas the buyer pays. In other areas the seller pays. And in yet other areas it's split between them, though not necessarily in half. Check with an agent to find out what's customary in your area.

Of course, there's nothing to prevent you from demanding that the other party to the transaction pay for the title insurance. In fact, it can be written in as a contingency of the deal. If you're lucky, the seller of the home you're buying and the buyer of the home you're selling will pay.

However, don't expect things to work that way very often. Real estate transactions are money deals. Title insurance can be translated at the time the deal is made to a specific amount of money, say $750. You want the other party to concede that much money. If you're a buyer, you're offering $750 less for the house. If you're the seller, you're asking $750 more. The other party can accept or can refuse. If they accept, however, they may reduce or raise the price accordingly to compensate. For example, you want the seller to pay for title insurance at a cost of $750. The seller agrees, but insists you pay $750 more for the home. What have you gained? (You may have gained something in the sense that you've converted a cash bill to one that can be mostly financed as part of the mortgage.) How it all comes out simply depends on how good a negotiator you are.

Can I Get the Title Insurance Company to Reduce Their Fees?

Maybe. Often a title company will offer you a reduced fee if you buy a home and then resell it within a short time, say six months. The reason, they assert, is that there's less title searching work for them to do. They only have to go back to the last deal six months earlier. Further, the new title insurance limits the liability under the old policy.

·H·I·N·T· ·

If you're going to cut a deal, be sure you do it before you hire the title company. It has to be something such as, "I'll give you both deals if you'll give me a discount; otherwise, I'll go elsewhere." Once they begin work and you sign the initial documents, you're probably locked in to their regular rates.

Another and perhaps more important reason, I suspect, is that they simply want more business. They can get two deals instead of just one.

You also can offer them two deals if the other parties agree to let you decide which title company to use. Instead of one deal, offer them a purchase and a sale. Many title companies will cut you a discount in this case.

Can I Save Money on Escrow Charges?

Again it's a matter of offering two deals instead of one. You're offering the company two escrows and two fees. Ask them up front if they will cut you a discount.

In some areas of the country, attorneys handle the escrow part of the transaction. Their fees for this are already quite low and they may not be willing to cut them further.

In addition, if you're dealing with a national escrow or real estate company, the local employees may not be able to cut you much of a deal because they may be required to adhere to the company's standards. (This is particularly the case if either the escrow or the title company is in some way affiliated with one of the brokers involved in the deal, although this tie-in may eventually be outlawed by federal legislation.)

What about the Other Charges?

In addition to title insurance and escrow charges, as a buyer you almost certainly will be required to pay loan charges. As a seller there will be recording and other fees. In short, there can be a great many charges amounting to thousands of dollars involved in each transaction.

Is there any way to save on these? The answer is yes and no. Some of the charges are simply pass-throughs. For example, the county may charge recording fees that are simply passed on through to you. Someone has to pay them and because you're the one who's having the documents recorded, it's logically going to be you.

On the other hand, some fees are simply garbage. For example, the lender may charge $300 for preparing the documents. Document preparation amounts to tapping a couple of keys on a computer. And in any event, it should be the lender's expense, not yours.

For the remainder of this chapter, we'll look at fees that are likely to be charged in real estate transactions and see which, if any, you may want to dispute.

Mortgage Fees Typically Charged to Buyer

Usually only buyers pay mortgage charges because, they are, after all, getting the mortgage. Sometimes, as discussed in Chapter 3, the lender will levy a prepayment charge against the sellers who are paying off a mortgage.

As a buyer, you should be given a good-faith estimate of charges as soon as you apply for a mortgage. This is required under RESPA (Real Estate Settlement Procedures Act). However, a few lenders in recent years have taken to grossly underestimating charges and even to not listing some charges. Because RESPA is loosely enforced, if at all, the consumer has suffered. You also should receive a statement at the time of closing (or within one day) of your actual closing costs (settlement charges).

Obviously the time to dispute the charges is when you first apply for a mortgage. Virtually your only leverage is that you can choose to look elsewhere if you don't like the deal a lender is offering. If you wait until the actual closing, you have lost your leverage. If you go looking for a new lender at that time, you stand an excellent chance of losing the deal. Because of the time it takes to process a mortgage, almost no seller will likely put up with such a delay.

Here are some of the mortgage fees you may run into, what they are, and whether you are likely to get them eliminated or discounted.

Application fee.   This charge, for applying for a mortgage, is garbage and should be treated as such. If you're charged an application fee, simply walk away and apply elsewhere.

Appraisal fee.   The charge for appraising the value of the home you are buying can sometimes be discounted if you have to have a reappraisal (if the initial appraisal was in error).

Attorney fees.   The charge for the lender's attorney to examine the documents is strictly a garbage fee. The lender should pay its own attorneys.

Credit report.   Normally you'll pay this charge for obtaining a credit report, but it only should cost around $50. Some lenders will refund this fee if you ask and eventually borrow from them.

Delivery fee.   This charge, for sending loan documents to the escrow company, may be as much as $150 or more. It's strictly garbage.

Document preparation.   This charge, for preparing the loan documents, is a garbage fee. The lender should pay for preparing its own documents.

Escrow mortgage fee.   This, a separate fee charged for handling the mortgage work in an escrow, is sometimes a garbage fee, unless actual extra work is involved.

Extra title insurance fee.   This charge, for a higher level of title insurance (ALTA) required by lenders, is a pass-through charge and is usually legitimate.

Homeowners/fire insurance.   This is the fee your insurance company charges for coverage. It's a legitimate fee.

Impound account setup fee.   If you are paying your taxes and insurance monthly, this is a charge to set up the account. If the charge is nominal, say under $50, it should be considered a legitimate fee.

Interest proration. This charge, for interest from the time you received the mortgage until your first mortgage payment, is legitimate. (Interest is charged in arrears so your first full monthly payment is usually one month after you've obtained the mortgage.)

Loan fee. This charge, for obtaining the mortgage, in most cases is a garbage fee.

Miscellaneous fees. These fees, for charges not specifically described, are strictly garbage fees. All charges should be specifically described.

Mortgage broker fee. This charge, for your mortgage broker's services, is probably a garbage fee because the lender should be paying the mortgage broker. In some cases, particularly involving second mortgages, the mortgage broker may reasonably charge you a fee for finding and securing the financing.

Notary fee. This charge, for notarizing the documents, is a garbage fee in that the escrow officer should notarize documents as part of the escrow service. However, if it's nominal, I wouldn't bother disputing it.

Points. A point equals 1 percent of the loan. Be sure that the points charged are the same as the points agreed on when you arranged for the financing.

Recording fees. The fees charged for recording your documents, as long as they are pass-throughs, are legitimate.

Storage or warehousing fee. This is the cost to the lender of holding the money ready for your mortgage until the day you fund. Typically this is only for a few days, but it's garbage anyhow. Today a lender can store money in an interest-bearing account and not lose out because it had to wait a day or two for you to be ready to fund.

Tax proration.   This charge is for taxes from the date due until you purchase the property. As a buyer you need to pay this proration.

Tax report setup fee.   This is a charge to an independent company that monitors your tax payments to be sure that you've made them (in cases where you don't pay them as part of your monthly payment). If you don't make the tax payments, they report this fact to the lender. This usually costs less than $35 and is a legitimate fee.

Title insurance.   As noted earlier, you may or may not have to pay this as a buyer, depending on local customs. It can be discounted.

Underwriting fee.   This charge an underwriter, such as Fannie Mae or Freddie Mac, makes to a lender for underwriting your mortgage should be the lender's, not yours.

As a seller, you also will face a number of charges. You should ask for a list of these fees as early on in the transaction as possible from your escrow officer. You may want to dispute these or ask for a discount. As with mortgage fees, your leverage comes from your ability to walk away and go to a different escrow company. But it's too late to do that on closing day. You must do it early on, preferably when you first select an escrow company.

Escrow Fees Typically Charged to Seller

Attorney fees.   These are fees to your attorney and you should have negotiated them up front. If they are to the escrow's attorney, they only should be for special services rendered.

Delivery fee.   The charge for sending documents by Federal Express or another similar service. Again, this should only be a pass-through fee and only if you have requested special service.

Document preparation.   If you have special documents prepared by the escrow, this is the fee. If it's just for looking at the documents sent by the mortgage company, it's garbage.

Escrow fee.   The charge for handling the escrow can sometimes be negotiated if you have two deals, as discussed earlier.

Home warranty package.   Typically the seller pays this, the cost of a home warranty plan for the buyer. It usually runs between $250 and $450.

Messenger fee.   The charge for delivering documents by special messenger can be very expensive, so try to handle everything through the mail or in person.

Miscellaneous fees.   These fees, for charges not specifically described, are strictly garbage fees. All charges should be specifically described.

Notary fee.   Some escrows include this charge for notarizing the documents in the service; others charge separately for each notarization. Try to avoid getting charged every time a notary stamps a document for you.

Recording fees.   These are pass-through fees for recording documents for you.

Tax proration.   This is the charge for taxes from the date due until the property is purchased. As a seller, you may receive money back if you've prepaid your taxes.

Title insurance.   This charge, for insuring title to the buyer, is negotiable.

Before the Deal Closes

Before the deal closes, you'll be asked to sign all sorts of documents, doubly so because you're involved in both a purchase and a sale. Read everything carefully. Question any charges you're not sure of. Question any statements or requirements you do not understand or do not agree with.

It's always a good idea to bring a real estate attorney with you to a closing. He or she can explain those items you don't understand and can give extra weight if you challenge any items.

Always do the math yourself, just to be sure. Yes, the escrow officer will point out it's done on their computers and it can't be wrong. But computers can fail on occasion. Remember, whether you're in buyer or seller mode, there's a lot of money involved, so be sure.

Take the time you need. Nothing happens until you sign. If you aren't sure, take the time to ask someone who can explain it to you. If you take overly long, the escrow officer will begin to complain. If you take even longer, the other party to the deal will complain. But ultimately, most of the time if you delay a reasonable amount, say a few hours, the results will only be complaints. Most people will give you the time to get it straight, so you understand it. (The exception is when there's is a limited time to fund a mortgage or some other issue is timely and you must sign before a deadline or the deal will not go through. If you fail to sign by the deadline, severe consequences could ensue.)

The Checklist: Saving Money When Closing the Deals

❏   1. Have you asked the title company for a discount?

❏   2. Have you asked the escrow company for a discount?

❏   3. Were you given a RESPA good-faith estimate of costs when you applied for a mortgage?

❏   4. Do you understand the difference between fair and garbage fees?

❏   5. Have you checked the list of fees to see if you're being charged any garbage fees?

❏   6. Are you ready to protest garbage fees to the lender before you go through the mortgage application process?

❏   7. Are you ready to protest garbage fees to the escrow officer before you open escrow?

❏   8. Do you understand why you may have to pay prorations?

❏   9. Have you asked a good agent or attorney to check over all your charges to see if they are legitimate?

❏ 10. Have you asked a good agent or attorney to look over your closing papers before you sign?

Finding a Builder Who Will Work with You

While most people opt to purchase "used" homes, about a million new homes are sold each year. Many of these do not go to first-time buyers. Rather, they are purchased by owners of existing homes who must sell in order to buy, presumably just as you do. Sometimes these new home buyers make spectacular deals with builders. Other times they make spectacularly bad deals. In this chapter we are going to look at ways to successfully negotiate the purchase of a new home and the sale of an existing home to a builder.

Whose Side Is the Builder On?

It's important to understand that builders are sellers of homes and just like individual sellers, they are out to get the best deal they can for themselves. However, unlike individual sellers, where your "adversary" is clearly defined, many times the builder appears to be on your side. This misconception is fortified by the typical aura surrounding new home sales.

When you decide to buy a new home, assuming you aren't buying a lot and building yourself, which is a different story, you typically will drive to a group of model homes. These have been built by a developer to show consumers what the actual houses (condominiums, townhomes, or other housing) that are offered for sale will look like when completed. Usually the model homes themselves are not for sale until the entire tract has been sold out.

You'll enter and typically be asked to "sign in" on a sheet that lists your name, address, and phone number. Most consumers assume that this is so that the builder can later send you brochures about the tract. (I've been through hundreds of new tracts, signed into all of them, and have seldom been sent a brochure or anything else from the builder at a later date.)

Actually, the reason you're asked to sign in is because this usually prohibits a real estate agent from later claiming a commission if you buy one of the new homes. The concept is that you saw the home first on your own (without an outside agent), so the agent of record is the builder (or whatever broker he employs). Thus, if you subsequently employ an agent to sell your existing home and then want to negotiate a deal for a reduced commission because of a buy-sell double deal, you won't be able to. Your selling agent probably won't be able to collect a commission (at least not a full commission) on the new home purchase.

·H·I·N·T· · · · · · · · · · · · · · · · · · · ·

If you want to work with an agent on the sale of an existing home, yet also buy a brand-new one, go with that agent to see the new home. In that case, the agent signs in for you and, assuming the builder is willing to pay a commission, as most are, you should be able to negotiate a discount with your agent.

Who Actually Represents Me with a Builder?

We're going to assume you don't want your independent agent to work with you, but instead you want to negotiate a complete deal with the builder. Therefore, you won't hesitate to sign in.

Typically you'll be greeted by the builder's agent, who will explain the layout of the tract, tell you the sizes and prices of the various models, give you a brochure, and urge you to walk through the homes. Later, if you decide to buy, this agent usually will be the one to draw up the sales agreement.

It's important to remember at all times that, in most cases, the agent who works at the model homes is the representative of the builder or developer. That agent's goal is to get the highest price and the best terms possible for the builder. No matter how much that agent may appear to be helpful to you, he or she is probably maintaining a fiduciary (loyalty) relationship with the builder or developer.

Therefore, if you go in alone, you're the only one truly representing you. You're on your own.

Should I Use an Independent Agent?

Should you negotiate with the builder directly or bring in an independent agent to do it for you (presuming you want the builder to take your house as a "trade-in" as described above)?

Having an agent on your side is always a good idea, particularly if you're not very savvy about real estate. So the question really comes down to who will pay the agent? Will the builder pay the fee, or must you?

·H·I·N·T············

In a "trade-in," you may get an agent to represent you for a fixed sum, say $1,000. This is more likely if the agent knows up front that all that he or she will be required to do is to handle negotiations and watch out for your interests during the completion of the deal. Nevertheless, many agents are unwilling to do even this for fear of liability if something should go wrong.

Some builders already have figured into their costs a selling commission for outside agents (typically half a full commission, usually 2½ to 3 percent). However, they may readily come down this much in price if don't work with an agent.

On the other hand, some builders intend to sell their property entirely on their own. This is often the case in a strong market. Which means that if you want an agent, you'll have to pay the fee.

Must I Pay Full Price?

This is why the builder's agents at model homes often present the properties as if they were selling cereal boxes in a grocery store. Model A is $135,000, model B is $157,000, and so on. Because it's written on a brochure, presumably you must pay the price that is asked.

Further, the builder or developer's agent often will insist on a very high deposit. And the terms of the transaction often will be prewritten in the agreement. In other words, you'll be told what the builder will accept. You'll have to take it or, the assumption goes, leave it.

Of course, this is all baloney. If one thing in life is true, it's that everything in real estate is negotiable. A builder or developer has homes to sell. If you can offer him or her a deal that makes sense (shows them some advantages), they'll take it. In other words, you can often negotiate not only the price of new homes, but also the terms, which are critical here.

An auto sales analogy is helpful. You walk into a new-car dealership and are shown a variety of models. Each has a sticker price plus whatever extras the dealer may have added. Do you assume that this is the real price?

In most cases (except for very popular cars), the sticker price is a fantasy. The actual price is lower, often thousands of dollars less. If you were to simply come in and pay sticker price, the salesperson would probably think you were from another planet.

Yet buyers often come into builders and pay the sticker price on homes. They don't question it. They don't try to negotiate.

What about the Sale of My Existing Home?

When you walk into a builder's model homes, you have your own special agenda. You not only want to buy a new home, you also want to dump your existing house. You want the whole round-trip, the full buy-sell process. And you want the builder to make it happen. In other words, you're after better terms than a straight cash purchase, which means that you need to negotiate.

·H·I·N·T · · · · · · · · · · · · · · · · · · ·

In real estate, negotiations typically occur on two levels—price and terms. If you want to get a lower price, you'll probably have to give up something on the terms. On the other hand, if you want better terms, you usually must be willing to pay full price. It's very rare that you can negotiate both better terms and a lower price.

What you want is for the builder to take your old home in trade on the new one. This is asking for terms. As such, my suggestion is that you worry less about the price of the new home, than about the terms you want. (You can make a better deal by doing some fancy negotiations on the price of your existing home, as described shortly.)

Why Would the Builder Take In My Old Home on Trade?

Let's go back to the analogy of a new-car dealership. Why would a new-car dealer be willing to take in used cars in trade? The main reason is that the dealer wants to move the new cars and most new-car buyers are also used-car sellers. Therefore, the dealer makes trades in order to sell his or her product, new cars. Along the way the dealer also makes a market in used cars.

New homes aren't that much different. Builders realize that in most cases, you have to sell your existing home in order to buy a new one.

That's why one of the first questions an agent will ask when you visit the new model homes is, "Have you sold your existing home?" If you answer yes, you've sold it, or it's in escrow, the agent's attention will immediately increase. You're a bona fide buyer. You are (or soon will be) able to buy the new home for a cash deal. You're the best type of buyer for the builder, because you offer a clean deal.

However, builders have a new outlook these days, based largely on market conditions. A decade ago builders were putting up tracts with hundreds, sometimes thousands of homes and selling them as fast they were built. Those builders acted in quite an independent manner. They demanded full asking price and often raised their prices on a monthly basis. They would never consider taking in a home on trade. They didn't have to; there were too many cash buyers.

Then came the real estate recession of the early 1990s and the attitude of builders changed. Instead of long lines of buyers (sometimes waiting days for a chance at a new home), there were no buyers at all. New homes languished while builders were making huge interest payments on them. Suddenly the idea of taking a trade made a lot more sense and builders were working all kinds of deals.

Then real estate came back in the late 1990s and once again builders saw good times. However, this time around they all realized that the good times would not last forever and they wanted those new homes sold, fast, before the next real estate recession hit. So many continue to negotiate with buyers.

Your goal is not only to find a new home builder whose homes you like, but a builder who also will be willing to work a trade on your existing home. That way, in a one-stop shopping situation, you can make the round-trip deal. You can buy and sell at the same time.

How Do I Get a Builder to Consider Trading In My Old Home?

Do it the old fashioned way—ask.

In some cases, the builder's agent will immediately say that, yes, the builder does offer a trade-in program and will then ask you if your home is currently listed. This is an important question, because if your home is listed, the builder will have to pay at least part of a commission to an outside agent. This seriously weakens what you have to offer and many builders at this point will simply bow out, saying they'll wait until you sell and won't consider a trade.

On the other hand, if you haven't listed your property at the time you talk to the builder, you've got a much better deal to offer. The builder not only won't have to pay a commission to an outside agent, but may be able to get a commission himself or herself on the sale of your existing home.

What happens next determines how good or bad a deal you will negotiate. Typically the builder's agent will want you to immediately list your existing home with him or her. The agent will say that the best way to get things rolling is to get your home listed and on the market.

Resist all tendencies to sign a listing agreement at this stage. If you sign a listing agreement before you negotiate a purchase with the builder, you've simply listed your house and tied yourself to the builder's agent. Now you'll have to sit and wait until your home sells before you can buy the new home.

Instead, explain that you want a solid purchase agreement on the new home and sale agreement on the old. And once that's tied down, you'll be happy to trade in the old property. Hopefully, you'd like the builder to take title to your old home so you can be done with it. You don't want to list it. You want the builder to buy it.

Will the Builder Actually Buy My Old Home?

Not unless he or she absolutely has to. Consider this: The builder starts out selling a brand-new home. After concluding the deal you want, he or she ends up selling a resale. Think of the automobile analogy. The dealer starts out with a new car and after making a deal now has to sell a used car.

However, with cars it's a bit different. Junkers can be wholesaled by the dealer and quality used cars can be sold on the dealer's own lot. There's no wholesaling houses and the builder is in competition with everyone when trying to sell a used home. It's a much worse situation for the builder.

But that's only if the builder actually purchases your home. Here are four different scenarios of what could happen:

1. The builder will want you to list (often with him or her) and put your home up on the market. You'll purchase but not move into the new home while you continue to make payments on the old until it's sold. Then your old mortgage will be paid off and funds from your equity for the down payment will be transferred to the builder and you'll move into some new one.

2. The builder will want you to list (often with him or her) and put your home up on the market. You'll buy and move into the new home and make payments on it while you continue to make payments on the old, until it's sold. However, the builder will guarantee that after a set time period, say 90 days, the builder will pick up the payments on it if your house hasn't sold. However, you'll have to agree to drop your price, sometimes substantially, at that time. When it does sell, of course, your equity will be cashed out. Remember, if the builder begins making your payments, you'll have to agree to reprice the home to the builder's demands; in other words, lower your price.

3. The builder will want you to list (often with him or her) and put your home up on the market. You'll buy and move into the new home and make payments on it while you continue to make payments on the old, until it's sold. However, after a set period of time, say 30 to 90 days, if your home hasn't sold, the builder will buy it at the full sales price (less commission).

4. The builder will buy your home outright and cash out your equity, which will be transferred to the purchase of the new home. It will be a clean deal.

It's important to note that unlike deals with automobile dealerships, you often retain ownership in your old home, and a liability on the mortgage for some time after the purchase of the new home. You probably will need to make some payments, the amount of your equity you realize after the sale will vary depending on the sales price, and you won't really be out from under it all until a true sale of your old home takes place.

Is the Time for Sale Critical?

Regardless of the type of deal the builder wants on a trade in, you may have to make double payments for a period of time. Therefore, it's to your advantage to have the time period during which you're responsible for payments be as short as possible. On the other hand, the builder wants it to be as long as possible.

It really all comes down to how long it should take to sell your home. You can be quite sure that builders know exactly the average time it takes to sell a home in your area. And they aren't likely to give you any breaks there. If homes are selling within 60 days, they'll want 90, just to be sure. If they're selling in 90 days, they'll probably want 120. In short, they want to be sure that the house really will sell during the time you're making the payments.

·**H**·**I**·**N**·**T** ·

Sometimes, if you're strapped for funds, the builder will make the payments on your old home and then subtract them from your equity when the house sells.

Why All the Hassle?

Why doesn't the builder simply buy the old home every time? It's the financing. Remember, in almost all cases homes are financed. And those loans contain "alienation clauses" that say the loan has to be paid off if you sell the house. Therefore, if title transfers to the builder, he or she must now pay off your existing loan and get a new one.

That's difficult for most builders. They are often already leveraged to the hilt to finance their new homes. They may not be able to finance an old home, too. The exception are some builders who have significant lines of credit and, for a short time, may be willing to transfer title, and if necessary, pay off your existing financing.

Who Decides on the Price of the Old Home?

That, of course, is the big question. You want your house to sell for as much as possible, thus giving you maximum equity. The builder wants the house to sell as low as possible, ensuring a quicker sale. The negotiations for how much to price your property are often the key to the entire buy-sell agreement.

·**H**·**I**·**N**·**T**· ·

Sometimes the builder will say that he or his agent will go by the house and appraise it. In other words, they will come up with a figure as to value. Don't accept such an offer. It's like asking the fox to hold the keys to the chicken coop.

In Chapter 11, we'll go into accurate home pricing so you can know exactly what your home is worth. Once you've done that, you can bring out the list of comparables and show them to the builder, backing up your estimate of value. Often, if a builder sees that you've done your homework and it checks out, he or she may go along with you.

Alternatively, the builder may insist that the home be formally appraised. He or she may suggest an independent agent to conduct an appraisal.

Be aware that an agent's appraisal is probably of no more value than your own. Indeed, it may be of less value because he or she may not spend as much time evaluating your property as you do.

If you agree to a professional appraisal, be sure it's handled by a true appraiser, one who does nothing else for a living and appraises properties for mortgage lenders. Ask that the appraiser belong to a professional organization such as the American Institute of Appraisers, whose members have the MAI designation.

Also be sure that before you sign anything there's a clause in the contract that says that if the appraisal comes out too low, in your opinion, you don't have to continue with the deal.

How Much Equity Will You Get out of Your Old House?

Again, let's go back to the analogy of selling automobiles. I've found that when buying a new car, the only time I really feel confident about knowing the actual price I'm paying is when it's a cash deal to the dealer. If it's a trade-in, so many figures get involved that I'm not sure if the big discount the dealer is giving me on the new car isn't off-set by the big hit I'm taking on the price of the trade-in. Trading homes with a builder can be a bit like that.

When you sell your old home outright (without a trade involved), you'll know exactly how much cash you'll get out at the time the deal is made. Not necessarily so in a builder's trade. Remember, the price determines your equity. But you may be required to lower your price if your house doesn't sell fast enough. Further, you may find your equity eroded if mortgage payments (and other costs) are deducted from the equity.

Of one thing you can be assured: The builder will go to great pains to ensure that you have enough remaining in your equity to purchase the new home. If it's 10 percent down, the builder will be sure that you have at least that much equity left, or else the deal might not be made. Of course, whatever is left of your equity (if anything) after you pay the down payment on the new property plus closing costs (which can be substantial) will be given to you.

What Can I Do to Better Control the Transaction?

If you're fairly savvy in real estate transactions, you shouldn't have any more difficulty in a builder's trade than in a straight sale. On the other hand, if this is a bit new to you, then I suggest you enlist the aid of a good real estate agent or attorney to look out for your interests and especially to explain the ramifications of all the documents you will be asked to sign.

The cost for these services varies but, as noted earlier, real estate attorneys, particularly on the East Coast, typically will handle all the work in a transaction for under $1,000, a terrific bargain considering the cost of legal services in other areas.

Who Actually Holds Title to the New and Old Properties?

This can be confusing. As noted earlier, the builder probably won't want to take title to your old property for fear of triggering the alienation clause. On the other hand, the builder won't want to give you title to the new home until you've secured a new loan and come up with the down payment. Thus, in some cases, you'll hold title to your old house and the builder to the new one until the complete sale goes through.

On the other hand, the builder is also anxious to get out from under the payments on his or her construction loan. So he or she may "credit" you with the down payment from your existing house and have you qualify for and get a mortgage on the new home. (This has the added advantage to the builder of knowing for sure that you can afford to buy the new home.) Thus, you may actually end up, at least temporarily, with title to both properties!

·H·I·N·T · · · · · · · · · · · · · · · · · · ·

In many cases, the builder won't allow you to move into the new home until either you've gotten a new mortgage and closed the purchase, or you've been fully preapproved by a lender.

However, you can be assured the builder will protect himself, possibly by having you sign a contract turning over the old house to him or her (perhaps in the form of a land contract of sale). However, the builder may not record that contract for fear of triggering the alienation clause. In theory, an unscrupulous buyer might be able to sign an unrecorded contract with the builder and then sell the old house out from under him. Just rest assured anyone who tries that will find themselves spending more time in court for the following few years than they'd ever care to.

Should I Get a Mortgage from the Builder's Lender?

There's also the matter of where you get the mortgage for your purchase of the new home. Invariably the builder will say that he or she has already arranged for financing of the new homes. The builder has contracted with a lender who's already appraised the property for full value and is ready to make a loan, provided you qualify.

However, just as invariably when I check out the terms of the mortgage the builder's lender is offering, it often seems to be at a higher-than-market interest rate, with more points and unfavorable terms (such as a prepayment penalty).

You don't have to use the builder's lender. You can use any lender you'd like. I suggest you go with one who offers you a legitimate market rate, few to no points, and no unfavorable terms. Simply tell the builder you'll arrange your own financing.

Strangely, when I've tried that at new homes, the agent representing the builder on occasion can be adamant that such an arrangement won't work. I have heard excuses such as, there isn't time for a new appraisal, the builder only works with the one lender, you'll have lots of extra paperwork and cost going with an independent lender, and so on.

While I can understand that a builder will feel more comfortable with a lender that already knows the property, I can't help but wonder why the strong insistence? Won't the property appraise out by an independent appraiser? (And if it won't, do you really want to pay that price?) Is there some sort of financial arrangement between the builder and the lender? (And if there is, aren't you paying for it?)

Money is money. My suggestion is that you always compare the interest rate, points, and terms the builder's lender offers with independent lenders—and then go with whoever offers the best financing deal for you.

What about Upgrades, Special Purchases, and Changes in Plans?

One last time, let's go back to the automobile purchase analogy. When you buy a new car there are almost always extras. Perhaps you want the leather trim, or the sports package, or the bigger engine. Dealers usually will have a list of available options, and their cost.

The key to getting a good new-car deal with regard to the extras is to have them included in the price. In other words, determine exactly what you want on the car you're buying before you negotiate price. If you wait until afterward, then you'll end up paying full retail for the extras, which are often offered at a very inflated price.

The same holds true with a new home. You'll be shown a model home, which often is filled with extras (although these days the extras are normally marketed plainly as options). You can buy the standard home, for which the builder has an asking price. Or you can add to the home extras from a list that might include:

- Upgraded carpeting
- Extra mirrors
- Special countertops in bath and kitchen
- Upgraded flooring in kitchen and baths
- Skylights
- Upgraded appliances
- Bigger lot
- Better located lot
- Fencing
- Landscaping
- The list goes on and on

I know my tendency, and that of most people, I suspect, is to concentrate on the main goal, the home itself. "I'll sweat the little things later," is what many people say. However, to do so is the same as to wait until after you've concluded a deal with a car salesperson and then ask for additional options. It costs much more.

Let's take carpeting as an example. Typically a standard home will come with inexpensive wall-to-wall carpeting. However, when you see the actual carpeting you'll get (not the upgraded version in the model home), you may quickly realize that it's not just inexpensive, but downright cheap. It looks bad and probably will wear out shortly. Therefore, you want to upgrade to better carpeting.

Typically you'll be told that you can go to a showroom where the various upgrades are available. However, you may be told that you must buy only from this showroom, because the quality of carpeting is tied into the lender's appraisal of the home and the city building department's approval of plans (not the case with carpeting). The trouble is that you find that the carpeting offered may be much higher priced than you could purchase it for independently.

There are two ways to handle this. One, you can decide on what carpeting upgrade you want, figure out what it should reasonably cost, and add that to the price you were planning to offer for the property. When you make your offer, simply write in that it includes such and such carpeting. If the builder accepts it, you've purchased the carpeting at a reasonable price.

The other way is to say that you'll buy the home without carpeting and you want the price of standard carpeting (it's usually priced so that you can subtract it from the cost of the upgrade), deducted from the price. You'll install your own carpeting.

There is a legitimate problem with this. The lender normally won't fund your mortgage until all the flooring is installed. That means that you'd have to install it and pay for it before you actually got title to the property. If anything screwed up the deal and it didn't go through, you would have paid for some wonderful carpeting in the builder's home. (Once installed, it becomes part of the home—you can't get it uninstalled.)

A solution may be a contract in which the builder will compensate you if, for some reason, the deal doesn't go through. However, most builders only will pay you the cost of the standard carpeting, which could be much less than your true cost for the better stuff you have installed on your own.

All of which is to say that you're usually better off going with the builder's upgraded carpeting, but negotiating the price as part of the purchase agreement.

By the way, you also may want to make certain changes in the design or layout of the home. Don't. Almost always the builder's plans have been approved as you see them by the local building department. A few options may be included. But making new changes requires going through the entire plan approval process again. Almost universally, builders will refuse to do this, with good reason.

Yes, it is possible to conduct a complete buy-sell transaction with a builder. However, it's certainly not going to be the easiest of transactions. Be prepared for a lot of negotiating and a lot of hardballing on the part of the builder. After all, the builder does this for a living, you're just doing it on a one-shot basis.

Find out how many homes the builder has fully finished, yet not sold. Remember that the builder is paying interest on the construction loans of each of these. If there are only a few, or none, you've got a builder who probably won't be willing to budge much, if any at all. On the other hand, if the builder has dozens of unsold homes, those interest payments could be eating him alive. In the lingo of the trade, he may be "highly motivated" to make a deal with you, even one that favors your interests.

The Checklist: Finding a Builder Who Will Work with You

❏   1. Do you understand that a builder is just another seller?

❏   2. Do you realize that the agent at the model home usually represents the builder, not you?

❏   3. Will you want to use your own agent to deal with a builder?

❏   4. Are you going to be careful about "signing in" at model homes?

❏   5. Are you clear about why and how to negotiate price and terms with a builder?

❏   6. Have you gotten the builder to take in your home on trade?

❏   7. Will you resist listing your home with the builder until you get a firm purchase contract on your new home?

❏   8. Are you prepared to make double payments, if necessary?

❏   9. Do you know when, if ever, the builder will buy your home?

❏ 10. Do you know what the actual sales price of your home is going to be when you trade?

❏ 11. Do you know when the sale will occur?

❏ 12. Do you know when you will be allowed to move into your new home?

❏ 13. Are you sure you will get all of your equity out of your old home?

❏ 14. Do you know whether you will want to use the builder's lender or your own?

❏ 15. Have you included upgrades in the purchase agreement?

Pricing It to Sell

While we've made a point of emphasizing that the buy-sell process is really a juggling act, with you needing to keep a variety of things in the air all at once, when you come right down to it, the basic holdup on the deal is always going to be your old property. Get it sold and everything else will begin to fall neatly into place. In this chapter we're going to see how to expedite the sale of the existing property. We're going to see how you can get a fast sale in virtually any market.

·H·I·N·T· · · · · · · · · · · · · · · ·

Don't think that by getting a fast sale you should simply sit and wait for the deal to close before going forward with the location and purchase of a new home. As we've noted, you need to coordinate many things almost simultaneously, including locating a new home, getting approved for new financing, working with an agent on a reduced commission, and so on. (If you're not sure about any of this, reread Chapter 2.)

157

What Most Determines the Speed at Which a Property Will Sell?

A host of factors determines how fast you can sell your property, including the following five items:

1. Location of your home
2. Market condition (Is it weak or strong?)
3. Size and layout of the home
4. Condition and "showability" of the property
5. Special financing terms you can offer

The one item you can most control is not on this list—price. Nothing determines speed of sale in real estate like price (after you've taken into account location), although this statement needs both clarification and qualifying.

What I mean when I say that price sells is that once you've factored in all of the above five influences, particularly location, you'll arrive at a range of prices. For example, homes with similar locations, sizes, conditions, and financing may be selling at between $110,000 and $125,000, or between $365,000 and $390,000, and so on. There are almost always two numbers indicating the highest sales price and the lowest sales price in the area. How quickly your house will sell usually lies somewhere between the two.

Price your house at the high end and you can expect it to sit there for some time before you eventually find a buyer. Price it at the low end and you can expect it to move more quickly. Which brings us to the question of just how you determine the price range for your house.

What Is My House Worth?

How do you determine the value of your home? I don't mean what is it worth to you. If you're like most people, it's probably worth much more to you than it ever will be worth to a buyer. The question is, what is it worth to a buyer?

While there are many methods of determining the value of a property, most home appraisers use the comparison approach. (Other methods include the cost approach, which bases price on cost of reproduction and the return-on-capital approach used for investment property.) Find out how much a comparable property sold for and that's the most likely value of yours. This is the method that mortgage appraisers, agents, and others involved in real estate use most often to determine the true value of a home.

It's easy to use. All you need do is find homes just like yours in your neighborhood that sold over the past six months to a year. You determine their sales prices and that creates a range. For example, you may find that over the past 12 months there were seven sales with a range of $170,000 to $193,000. Chances are your house is worth somewhere in that range.

Should I Check Out the Comparables?

What you now must do is to check the comparables to see why some were more expensive and others less. Did the most expensive home have a swimming pool? Was the least expensive a "fixer-upper" in terrible shape (also called a "handyman's special")? Often you can determine the reasons homes are placed where they are in the price range.

Keep in mind that you don't actually have to go to each of these properties physically to check them out (although you may want to drive by to see if a better curb appeal on one than another was a factor). You can do your checking in your agent's office.

Almost all listing services across the United States are computerized. That means that an agent should be able not only to give you a list of comparable sales in your area, but also to pull up each listing, which gives a detailed description of the home. By examining the listings, you should be able to tell quickly which homes were really much like yours and which had more or fewer amenities and features.

You should pay special attention to items such as the following:

- Square footage (the larger, the more valuable the property)
- Swimming pools and spas (which add value)

- Number of bedrooms (At least three is considered necessary; more is better, provided there's enough square footage to accommodate them; two or fewer reduce value.)
- Number of baths (At least two is considered necessary; more is usually better; less reduces value.)
- Special extras, such as a fireplace or chef's kitchen, that may have added value
- The condition of the property. Often there are messages on the listing suggesting the condition of the property. (The terms *fixer-upper* or *handyman's special* or *needs TLC* usually indicate a home in poor shape.)

Can I Use a Comparison Sheet?

Whenever I've attempt to do a comparison of homes in an agent's office, I usually discover that I can't keep track of the various factors involved in the properties. I find that while one has a pool, another an extra family room, yet another is a fixer-upper, and so forth. It's hard to remember which is which. Therefore, I use a quick comparison sheet to help me. I've included a copy in Figure 11.1 so it may be of help to you, also.

The whole point behind the comparison sheet is to help determine if a comparison house had added value because of a special feature that yours doesn't have. If it does, then you can't use the price of that house as an indicator of the value of yours until you compensate for that factor. You must subtract the value of the special feature to find the true worth of your home.

Using this comparison method, you should be able to quickly determine just how much your home is worth based on recent sales. As I noted, this is your best indicator of value.

FIGURE 11.1 • Quick Comparison Sheet

	Prop. 1	Prop. 2	Prop. 3	Prop. 4	Prop. 5
Address					
Square footage					
Bedrooms					
Baths					
Family room					
Garage					
2 car					
3 car					
Pool					
Spa					
Fireplace					
Hardwood floors					
Air-conditioning					
Good front yard					
Heavily traveled street					
Suggested condition					
Added value					
Reduced value					

To use this comparison sheet, simply enter the addresses of each property in the first row. Then fill out the information in the column below. *Note:* It's not necessary to fill out all the cells. For example, if all the homes but one have three bedrooms and that one has four, simply put a +1 in that cell and you'll know what the added feature was.

What If I Disagree with the Comparison Results?

One of the unspoken pastimes in most neighborhoods is loosely tracking housing values. Any time a nearby house sells, we usually try to learn the sales price. After all, that lets us know what our house might be worth. However, for many of us this process is selective. When we learn that a nearby house has sold for more, we add to the value of our own home. However, when prices decline and a nearby house sells for less, we tend to dismiss that lesser sale as a market aberration. In other words, most of us add value when the market goes up, but don't subtract value when the market goes down. Thus our own "guesstimates" of our home's value may be far from accurate.

It's important to understand that the market doesn't care how much you paid for your home; how much money, tears, and sweat you put into your home; how much you owe on your mortgage; or even how much your home was worth three years ago. All the market cares about is what a buyer is ready, willing, and able to pay right now. And that you should have discovered from comparing other sales.

Should I Pay Attention to Listing Price versus Sales Price?

Thus far we've been talking exclusively about sale prices. However, in most market conditions a home is listed for more than it eventually sells for. Buyers make offers and the home sells for less. How much less depends on a multitude of conditions, including how strong the market is, how desperate the sellers are, and so on. For example, in one market the difference between sales and listing prices might be 5 percent. In another market it might be 2 percent. In yet another, 7 percent. Once again, an agent should be able to give you the average figure. If not, you easily can figure it out yourself, because the listing sheets should show both sales and listing prices.

•**H**•**I**•**N**•**T**• •

Be careful never to ask for a price higher than the value range of your home. To do so will almost certainly guarantee that you'll wait a very long time for a buyer to come by.

If you know the sales figures and then you list at those figures, you won't have any margin to play with. Most buyers will assume you anticipate that they will offer less than you're asking, and you'll be hit with a lot of what appear to be lowball offers. Don't take these—wait.

To avoid lowballs, most sellers add on a certain percentage to their anticipated sales figures (usually the average amount for their area or for the comparables they have used). Thus, if you figure your house is worth $114,000 based on *sales* figures, you might ask $120,000, knowing that you'll come down $6,000 to a buyer. However, at that price you're not offering much of a bargain.

How Much Must I Lower My Price to Create a Bargain?

It's important to understand that if you've correctly priced your home based on comparables, it should sell. The only question now is how long it will take. You actually can get this information from an agent.

Most listing services, in addition to offering information on listings, also compile overall information and one of these, that's always available, is the average time to sell. The time to sell is typically given in days. Based on an average time it's taken for previous listings to sell, it could take 37 days, 90 days, 185 days, or whatever. It's an ongoing and ever-changing figure.

The time-to-sell figure means that if you're willing to wait, which you may be, you reasonably can expect your home to sell within the average time-to-sell time frame, assuming it's priced accurately. This doesn't guarantee it will sell, but it's usually a pretty good indicator.

On the other hand, perhaps you want to sell sooner. As we all know, time is money. If you want to shorten the time, you have to give up some of the money. The question now becomes, how much?

There are several ways to look at this. The approach most quoted is the qualification pyramid. Homebuyers must be able to afford financing. The higher the price, the fewer buyers available to purchase that home. The lower the price, the more buyers in the pool.

For example, a home priced at $135,000 (close to the median price nationwide) in a given area might be affordable by 50 percent of buyers. A home at $200,000 in the same area might be afforded by only 15 percent. Raise that price to $400,000 and only 2 or 3 percent of buyers might be able to afford it. Thus, the argument goes, by lowering the price you increase the number of buyers who can afford your property.

In other words, there's a pyramid of potential buyers who can qualify for a home. At the top, where there are very few, are the high-priced homes. At the bottom, where many can qualify, are the lower priced homes.

But does that translate into a speedier sale? In our example, the home in the $400,000 price range might actually be sold overnight by dropping the price to $350,000, even though less than 3 or 4 percent of buyers in that area could afford it at that lower price. Does increasing the number of potential buyers by only 1 percent induce such a quicker sale?

I don't think so. What makes the sale speedier is the fact that the lower price is perceived as a bargain. In the example, I noted that dropping the price $50,000 on a $400,000 home would almost surely ensure a quick sale. But it might be possible to drop the price much less, say 5 percent ($20,000) and get a sale almost as quickly. Or drop it even less, say 2 percent ($8,000) and hasten the time it takes to get a sale. A lot depends on the price range, which we discussed earlier. If you can drop your price down to the bottom of the range for homes such as yours, you will be offering what many buyers perceive as a bargain.

For example, if the asking price range for your home is between $110,000 and $125,000 and you offer it for sale at $110,000 (or as a teaser, $109,000), you'll catch buyers' interest. You'll be offering your home for less than any other home in the area was offered in the recent past. It will seem like a bargain. (But, as noted, you'll have to contend with lowball offers.)

Will Buyers Respond to My Bargain Price?

Yes, they will. This was brought home to me once when I was doing a radio talk show on the East Coast. A caller asked how he could market his home, which had languished without an offer for six months, more quickly. I pointed out that he could market a home better by paying attention to its curb appeal and by offering better terms. A real estate agent called in and said that I was overlooking the most important factor, price. All he had to do was lower the price and he'd get a sale. If he lowered it far enough, he'd get a sale the very next day, in any market.

Well yes, I countered, that's of course correct, but this seller couldn't lower his price below his existing financing, which was already near the sales price. He'd have to take money out of his pocket to sell the home if he went much lower. (Which is something people sometimes must do in a very bad market.)

Nonetheless, the agent was essentially correct. Lower your price and you'll find a buyer. Lower it a lot and you'll find that buyer very quickly.

How Do I Get Across to Buyers that I'm Offering a Bargain Price?

Selling a home is a numbers game. You want to get as many people out to look at your property as possible. The more who see it, the more likely one is going to like it and make an offer, especially if you're offering a bargain price.

On the other hand, if no one sees your property, it won't make any difference how much you lower your price. You still won't get any offers. Thus, it comes down to marketing. You must let buyers know that you've got a property for sale and that it's bargain priced.

How do you do that?

If you're selling FSBO (for sale by owner), it's hard. You'll want to advertise online, in the newspapers, by word of mouth, with flyers, on bulletin boards, and so on. If you've listed with a good agent, it's far, far easier.

Agents can "talk up" your property at their weekly regular board or association meetings, where most of the active agents gather to discuss real estate and listings. An agent can stand up at this meeting and say, "I've got a terrific listing. It's priced lower than any other house has sold for in the area in the last year. It's a real bargain!" In some areas a "hot sheet" is sent to agents containing similar information.

Of course, your agent is talking to other agents. But those other agents are scouting houses for clients. At any given time, perhaps 90 percent of all buyers are tied in with an agent. So your agent is really spreading the word where it counts.

If you're really interested in offering a bargain, you can help your agent by making a special offer. If you authorize it, your agent can stand up and say, "My sellers will offer the agent who brings in a buyer a ½ percent bonus on the commission." Because the commission is based on the sales price, this can be a sizable amount. Giving it to the agent instead of the buyer may help you get a faster sale.

Selling the Sizzle More Than the Steak

I'm sure many readers who aren't familiar with the way agents work are wondering if I'm serious about this procedure. I certainly am.

Your best shot of finding a buyer in your area is through the broker network. If you can tap into it, your home will get lots of attention. More important, if you can get the brokers excited about bringing buyers by to see your home (because of some incentive you've offered) you'll not only be tapping into the network, but making it hum.

And don't be shy about the offers! When the market is particularly slow, I've seen everything from TV sets to refrigerators to a second-hand car offered to agents!

If you want a quick sale, the best approach is to get agents excited about your house. They'll work hard for you, if they believe it will mean a quicker, bigger commission.

Will Buyers Offer Still Less, Hoping for a Bigger Bargain?

You've cut down your price to the lowest asking price that anyone has had on your particular model of home, given its location, for the past year. You've given agents incentives. And now you've got all kinds of potential buyers coming through. But, as noted, won't they offer still less than you're asking, hoping for an even bigger bargain?

Of course they will, unless it's an extremely hot market and they're concerned that there will be multiple buyers coming in with competitive offers. In that case they may offer full price or even more than what you're asking for the property! (In some hot markets I've seen five and six offers come in on the same day, all of them for more than the sellers were asking!)

In a slow market, you may get lowball offers, but you're not obligated to take a lower price than you're asking. What you want is activity. If you get enough offers coming through, chances are eventually one of them will be close to what you're asking and you may be able to negotiate the buyer up. Or you may find you're willing to take a little bit less to get the sale.

Are There Special Concerns on Pricing FSBOs?

If you sell by owner, you're presumably saving on the commission and have some room to play with. So give the buyers an even bigger price discount, and you will sell your house faster and may even net more money.

Remember, with FSBOs, you're not offering an advantage to buyers, but a disadvantage. Most buyers would prefer to deal with an agent than a seller. They're afraid to tell you to your face what they really think about your property and what they'd like to offer. So, they don't tell you and many don't offer. On the other hand, they're usually more than willing to speak openly to an agent and make offers through an agent.

The quickest way to overcome this disadvantage is to lower the price. The mistake that most of those who sell FSBO make is thinking that they can keep the whole commission savings for themselves. You can't do that and realistically expect to sell the property in short order. Instead, you have to at least split the commission you're saving with the buyer by offering a lower price. If you've appraised your home correctly and then discount it even further (using the money you save on the commission), you'll have an extremely attractive bargain. And buyers will sniff it out.

Buyers who might otherwise pass because of the inconvenience of dealing directly with a seller, will now be willing to tackle the hassle. You're suddenly the best deal in your price range.

Remember, you're interested in selling quickly, not just in saving money by going FSBO. If you're interested in a quick sale, you have the perfect opportunity with a FSBO because you can offer to sell for so much less than your neighbors who are listed through an agent.

How Quickly Can I Realistically Expect to Sell?

That depends on how carefully you follow the rules. If you price your property correctly and promote it either through an agent or, as a FSBO, by yourself, you'll get a quick sale.

I've sold my own homes both ways, and over the course of more than 30 years and more homes than I care to remember, I don't recall ever taking more than five weeks to find a buyer and lock in an offer. If I had to guess, I'd say that the usual time frame is between two and three weeks, and this has been in good markets and bad.

Remember, the key here is to check out the comparables to find the price range of your home. Then, if you want a quicker sale, go to the lower end of the price range, offer incentives to agents, and create a bargain. Price your property right and you'll have trouble keeping buyers away.

The Quiz: Pricing It to Sell

Yes   No

☐   ☐   1. Is price what most determines how quick your home will sell?

☐   ☐   2. Is your house worth what it cost you plus 5 percent a year appreciation?

☐   ☐   3. Is a *comparable* another house very similar to yours that recently sold?

☐   ☐   4. Is a comparison sheet useful in keeping track of comparables?

☐   ☐   5. For a quick sale, should you list for the lowest price a comparable recently sold for?

☐   ☐   6. Is having agents "talk up" your house an important part of getting buyers?

☐   ☐   7. Should you offer promotions to agents for finding a buyer?

☐   ☐   8. Can you save the whole commission if you sell FSBO?

☐   ☐   9. Does a FSBO attract more buyers and is it easier to sell?

☐   ☐   10. Can you offer a better deal to buyers as a FSBO seller?

Answers

1. Price is the single biggest factor you can control, after you've taken into account location.

2. Unfortunately, no. Your home is only worth what a buyer is ready, willing, and able to pay for it. In other words, it's only worth what the market will bear.

3. It certainly is.

4. Unfortunately, comparables are only similar, not identical. A comparison sheet helps to identify and account for the differences.

5. It's important to remember the difference between "list" price and "selling" price. Houses normally list for more than they sell. If you list for the price you want to sell, you won't have any wiggle room, but you'll be offering a bargain.

6. Agents can facilitate your sale, but only if they know about your property. Perhaps the biggest service your agent can perform is getting the word out to other agents.

7. It can't hurt and in a slow market, it's a definite help.

8. Yes you can. But it may mean that you'll take a very long time to sell.

9. It definitely attracts buyers who are looking for a bargain. But it's harder to sell because buyers are hesitant to deal directly with sellers.

10. Yes you can. You can cut your price by all or a portion of the commission you would otherwise pay, thus reducing your price below that of comparables.

Moving Headaches

It may seem as though finding a buyer for your old home and buying a new one are the big problems; everything else is a minor detail. However, once you get far enough along in the deal that you're down to the logistics of moving, the buy-sell may seem like the minor difficulty!

If both homes close on the same day, your moving problems will be minimized. But if there's a time break between the time you can move from the old and into the new, it can mean all kinds of difficulties. In this chapter we're going to look into how to minimize moving headaches by planning ahead.

When Is the Actual Move Date?

This can be difficult to nail down. Usually you only get possession after your new mortgage funds and escrow closes. Then the seller will hand over the keys and the property will be yours. Similarly, you won't be handing over your keys to the new owners of your old home until their mortgage funds and their escrow closes.

Knowing those dates (hoping they will be the same date) well in advance can take a bit of wizardry. Many factors can delay either escrow. You or the seller of the home you're buying may have a problem with the title, and that could delay the deal. You may need to complete repairs to correct termite damage or other problems in your home, or the one you're buying, and that could delay things. Either escrow could lose important papers. And so on.

Thus, while you may have set a deadline and may be aiming for that date, it would be judicious to make contingency plans, just in case one escrow or the other happens to be late in closing. Early planning here can not only save money, but also a lot of headaches.

·H·I·N·T ·

Occasionally an escrow is ready to close early. That's usually a good thing when you have two escrows to close. You simply hold up on the early escrow until the normal-speed (or late) one is ready. If you've allowed yourself enough time on both, the other party won't be able to object (see Chapter 8).

When Should I Arrange for the Movers?

It's a good idea to arrange for moving about 30 to 60 days before you're ready to close escrows. At certain times of the year, movers can be very busy and may have difficulty scheduling you in. This is particularly the case during the summer months. Also, it's much easier to get a mover if you want to move on a weekday than on a weekend.

Of course, you could always move yourself. If that's the case, you'll undoubtedly need to rent a moving truck from one of the many rental companies such as Ryder or U-Haul. Again, do it early, because their trucks are often spoken for weeks in advance, particularly during the summer months and on weekends.

My suggestion is that you reserve a date for either a truck or the movers on the date you anticipate your move will occur. If things don't work out as planned and you have to delay, it's usually a lot easier to change the date to a later one than it is to get a brand-new date on short notice.

You can find movers listed in the yellow pages of the phone book. Having used many, I've found that the quality of the movers (whether items get broken or lost) depends on the individual movers more than the moving company.

The cost of moving is regulated, so the rates are virtually the same and are based on weight. For a certain weight, you'll be charged a set rate in most cases by whichever company you use. Recommendations of different movers by people who have recently used them are helpful, but if you get the same company but different people, you could get a different result.

The big difference between companies that rent moving trucks tends to be the quality of the equipment, although on any given date the price also can vary enormously, depending on demand.

Call a couple of moving companies and you'll find they'll be happy to send an estimator to give you a bid. Just keep in mind that, as noted earlier, rates are regulated. All the estimator can do is give you an educated guess as to the weight you have and calculate a price on that. For the actual move, the moving truck will be weighed prior to coming to pick up your furnishings and then again once it's loaded. You'll be charged for the actual weight. When selecting a mover, also ask about storage, as noted later in this chapter.

What If the New Home Closes before the Old?

Closing on your new home a few days before you sell your old, as may happen, can be a godsend. You can get in there and clean and paint. And you can have your furniture moved at your leisure.

Of course, you may have to pay a few extra bucks for interest and taxes, but having the house at your disposal to fix up before you move in will surely be worth it.

What If the Old Home Closes before the New?

This can be a serious problem. Chances are that the buyers of your existing home will want you out on the day escrow closes. (If you're not out, you become a tenant and they will worry that you could stay there forcing them, as a last recourse, to evict you!)

Because your new home hasn't closed, you can't move unless you can convince the sellers of your new home to let you in early. If they're already out, they may be willing to do this and charge you rent for the time you're there. But don't count on it happening. If you move into the new home and, for any reason, the purchase doesn't go through, you become a tenant and they would worry that they'd have to evict you to get you out (in order to sell to someone else).

I have let buyers move in early to homes I was selling that were vacant, but not without misgivings. I've always insisted on a stern rental agreement and a big security deposit, just in case. That's what you would probably face if the sellers of your new home let you in early.

On the other hand, the sellers of your new home may be living in the property themselves. They can't move until the deal closes, so you can't move in. What do you do now?

The answer is storage. If you must move from your old home and can't yet move into the new home, you've got to store your furnishings (as well as find a place to stay for yourself). This can be very expensive, or cost virtually nothing at all, depending on your movers and the length of the delay.

Remember, the movers not only have to get your furnishings onto a truck, that truck has to transport them to your new home—and that takes time. Often it can take several days. If you have a small load and they combine it with another load, it can take a week or more.

Check with the movers in advance. Find out if it's possible for them to store your furnishings on the truck for a few days or longer in the event you can't move into your new home in a timely manner. They may be willing to do this for nothing or for a small fee.

On the other hand, if it's going to be a week or much longer, you may need to arrange for actual storage of your furnishings. Be sure you hire a mover who has a place to store your things on a short-term basis.

Unfortunately, this also can be quite expensive and you must pay for the off-loading from the truck, the storage, and the later on-loading. It's like having to move twice!

If at all possible, try to avoid having to store your furnishings with a mover because of the cost. Perhaps you can work out an arrangement with the buyers of your new home to temporarily store much of your things in your old home's garage for a few weeks. Most people are more than willing to help out, when they can.

Where Will I Stay If There's a Delay in Getting into My New Home?

The most expensive and often least appealing answer is in a motel. However, if you realize that delays are a possibility, you may be able to make other arrangements. By doing it well in advance, you may be able to arrange to stay for a short period with friends or relatives in the area. Many times people who you'd never thought would be willing, are gracious and will help you out.

If that doesn't work, you may be able to arrange for short-term housing (by the week) at a local apartment building or motel. Some will allow and even welcome this, but usually the arrangements, including a deposit, must be made well in advance.

What about Utilities?

The idea here is to coordinate the effort. Assuming that your old and new homes are relatively close to each other, you will want the utility companies to shut off service at the old and turn it on at the new on the same date. To have them accomplish this (which they will do) you must usually give them adequate notice, perhaps a couple of weeks.

My suggestion is that you make arrangements at least two weeks before your anticipated move. I've found it's much easier to call later and move the date back, if necessary, than it is to try to arrange for the transfer a few days before I want it done.

On the other hand, if you're moving out of the area, you must make double arrangements. Turning off utilities at your old home is no problem. Usually companies can do it with only a couple days' notice, although calling well in advance is advisable.

Arranging for service at your new home, however, again requires advance notice, at least two weeks. Go ahead and give the utility companies your arbitrary date. Once the utility has your name on its books and has okayed a date for turn on, it's a simple matter to call later and ask them to hold off for a day or two (or longer). Utilities are used to having such delays and handle them as a matter of course. What takes time is setting up your account. The utility will probably want time to verify credit information and may even require that you come down and put up a deposit. It can take anywhere from a few days to three weeks to initiate utility service. But, once your account is set up, it's only a phone call to have the turn-on delayed.

The utilities you'll need to contact include the following:

- Phone
- Electricity
- Gas
- Water
- Garbage service
- Cable service
- Newspaper delivery
- Pool/spa service
- Gardener
- Any other utility you will use in your area

Agents are usually very good in providing you with a list of numbers for the utilities. If not, the numbers are often contained in the front matter of the local phone book. You also can ask the seller what utilities are used. If all else fails, you can use the yellow pages of the phone book.

What If I Move into My New Home and the Sale of My Old Home Falls Through?

As noted in an earlier chapter, you might have to make up two mortgage payments for a time until you can resell. Or, if things get really tough, you may arrange for financing to bridge the gap between the two homes and then rent your old home out (see Chapter 7 for details).

A word about renting out your old home. You should not do this on a short-term basis, anything less than six months. For a short time, it's better to bite the bullet and pay double mortgage payments.

The reason is that it's inevitable that tenants will cause some damage and some wear and tear on your old home. This is particularly the case with short-term tenants (under six months) who may not feel any responsibility toward keeping your property in top shape.

Presumably it's ready to show to potential buyers right now. Chances are, however, that after tenants move out, you'll need to go in and spend time and money once again cleaning it up, repairing whatever's broken, and getting it ready to show.

By the way, put any thoughts out of your mind of trying to sell the property while there are tenants in it. This is the hardest sell of all.

When you're living in the home, you're ready to show the property to buyers at any time, day or night. And you're always keeping it in tip-top shape. You do this because it's to your advantage . . . you want it sold as quickly as possible so you can get your money out.

There's no advantage to renters for doing the same thing. For them, always keeping the property neat and clean is a burden. Showing it is a bigger burden.

I've seen situations where tenants have promised to cooperate with agents who want to show the property, but after a few days of being bothered by prospective buyers, they simply lock the doors and say, "No more!" They won't let anyone in and they're obstinate about it. You can't do anything until their rental term is up and you get them out.

If you do decide to rent out your home, be sure you get a hefty security deposit, an appropriate rent, and have the tenants sign a strong tenancy agreement. For more information on this, check into my book, *The Landlord's Troubleshooter* (Chicago: Dearborn, 1994).

What about Problems after the Sale or Purchase?

You move into your new home and you find the water heater leaks. Or there's a broken window. Or there's a crack in the foundation that the sellers never mentioned. And the agent of the buyers of your old home calls to say that the garbage disposal doesn't work (even though it did work dutifully for the past 11 years), or a fence is down, or the roof leaks.

What do you do?

If you have a home warranty package (both on your new home and on your old), it should take care of the little stuff such as a new water heater or garbage disposal. On the other hand, you'll probably have to pay to have the fence fixed and the sellers of your new home will have to pay for a new window, although homeowners insurance should cover the cost of both.

The real danger is with severe problems, such as a foundation crack or leaky roof. Both of these should have been covered prior to the sale in disclosures (see Chapter 8). If not, it becomes a sticky business. The sellers (of your new home and you for your old home) may be responsible. The buyers (of your old home and you for your new home) may eventually take the sellers to court to get appropriate repairs done, as well as seek damages.

My suggestion is that you be as realistic as possible about severe problems. You may not have known that the roof leaked because it didn't before. Or maybe you just forgot to mention it to the buyers. In either case, if it happens right after the sale, you may want to offer to pay for minimum repairs to close out the problem. If a new roof is required, or repairs are extensive and expensive, and the other party is persistent about you paying the costs, it's probably time to contact a lawyer. Even so, negotiating a solution will probably be quicker, less painful, and less costly than taking it all the way to court. Hopefully, the buyer of your old home will see it the same way.

The Checklist: Moving Headaches

☐   1. Do you have a tentative move date set?

☐   2. Will you arrange for the movers at least a month ahead of time?

☐   3. Will you arrange for a moving truck (if you're doing it yourself) at least a month before you need it?

☐   4. Have you made arrangements for possible furniture storage?

☐   5. Have you made arrangements for where you can stay, if you can't move into your new home on a timely basis?

☐   6. Have you called up for utility connections?

☐   7. Have you a contingency plan if the deal falls through on your old home and you go through with the purchase of your new one?

☐   8. Do you have home warranty plans on both properties?

☐   9. Do you know what to do if there's a minor problem with either home after the deals close?

☐ 10. Do you know what to do if there's a major problem?

Appendix

Don't Forget about Safety

Things to Check before You Sell *or* Buy

If you sell your existing home without smoke detectors and the first night it catches fire and the new owners are injured, would you feel responsible? If the home you buy has no fire detectors and catches fire the first night you're in it, would you feel that the sellers had shirked their responsibility?

Today, when you sell and buy property, you need to be concerned that the home is safe and has no obvious hazards. As a seller, besides allaying your own feelings of responsibility, there also could be financial and legal consequences if the home is unsafe. As a buyer, it's just not worth the risk to life and limb.

Of course, the question immediately arises: What *are* you responsible for? As a seller do you have to be sure that the house is fire safe? Do you have to be sure that the various systems, such as gas and electric, are safe? What if you've lived in the property for years and it's been okay, do you now need to suddenly make upgrades and changes?

As a buyer, can you rely on the seller to be sure that the house is safe? Or are there things you must do to protect yourself before you move in? We'll discuss the entire area of safety in this appendix.

When You Sell Your Existing Home

What we're dealing with here is basically your level of comfort. Are you comfortable simply disclosing a safety defect in a house you're selling? Does just telling the buyers about it make you feel that you're off the hook? In most states, simply disclosing a problem may be all that you are legally required to do. Most states also do not require you to correct these problems.

However, I don't feel comfortable just disclosing safety problems. For example, I recently sold a house with a swimming pool that had an electric light built into the pool's side wall. I had gotten a shock from the light once when I was in the water, so I made sure it was never turned on while I owned the property. Would simply telling the buyers about the probable defect allow me to rest easy at night?

No. I'd worry that the buyers would disregard what I had said, turn on the light, jump in the water, and possibly get electrocuted. Besides the moral concern, there was the very real concern that I might be held liable for what happened and could face civil action by relatives of the deceased, if not criminal charges.

Therefore, prior to the sale, I had the light removed and filled the space with decorative tiles. True, the swimming pool now had no light, which was a drawback, but it was not enough of a drawback to cause a potential buyer to refuse to make the purchase or even consider a reduced price offer. Simply by doing what was right, I eased my conscience and avoided a potentially serious financial problem in the future. My level of comfort was achieved by entirely removing the potential hazard.

When You're the Buyer

The seller may inform you that there's a safety problem with the property. For example, the pool light gives off shocks. What should you do?

You can demand that the seller fix the problem prior to closing escrow. But, can you trust the seller to fix the problem? Yes, if it's done by a professional. For example, if the pool light is fixed by an electrician, then presumably it has been done right.

The real problems remain when the seller doesn't mention a potential problem and you are left to discover it on your own. This is the reason to have an extremely thorough home inspection done *before* you move in. Make sure the inspector checks out such things as the pool light and gas lines, for instance.

Do States Regulate Safety Items?

Many states require that sellers certify certain safety equipment is in the property. California, for example, requires that every single-family dwelling sold after 1986 have an operable and approved smoke detector and that all water heaters be braced, anchored, or strapped to resist earthquake motion. If there is no operable smoke detector or the water heater is not strapped, the seller must inform the buyer of this.

Other states require a fire extinguisher on the property or that there be appropriate safeguards in the event of hurricane, tornado, or other natural disaster. To find out the state requirements in your area, check with a good real estate agent. He or she should be able to quickly fill you in on this vital information.

Beyond state requirements, there are commonsense safety requirements. Below, we'll look at what you as a seller should be concerned about when you sell, and what you as a buyer should look for when you purchase.

Is There a Fire Hazard?

There is always a chance of fire in any dwelling, no matter how fireproof it might appear to be. In fact, most modern housing is very fire resistant. The use of Sheetrock walls and taped joints will often prevent fires that begin in furniture from spreading beyond the room in which they start. Indeed, common home wallboard is rated in terms of how many minutes it can withstand a direct flame without passing the fire through to the other side. (Depending on the thickness, the time can be more than an hour!) Nevertheless, fires do start from freak accidents, and the issue becomes what reasonable safety features the house has to alert residents and to help extinguish the fire.

Smoke Alarms

At minimum, every house should be equipped with at least one smoke alarm. Ideally, there should be one on every floor, in the basement, and in every bedroom. They are inexpensive (often costing less than $15) and easy to install.

The biggest issue with smoke alarms seems to be whether they use batteries or plug into a 110-volt electrical system. There are arguments that favor both sides of this question. For example, many people correctly point out that often the first system in the house to fail in a fire is the electricity. It could short out, meaning that the smoke alarm would be inoperative and would fail to waken sleeping occupants.

On the other hand, many building departments point out that the biggest single cause of failure from smoke alarms is dead batteries. Thus, when there's a fire, the device fails to operate.

Check the requirements in your area. Some building and safety departments insist on alarms that attach to the home electrical system. Others insist that they be battery operated.

My own approach is to avoid taking any chances by purchasing both types. In every home I sell or buy, I am sure that there's both a battery-operated alarm (with fresh batteries) and one plugged into the home's electrical system. Better safe than sorry!

Fire Extinguishers

A fire extinguisher in a kitchen as well as one in the garage is a good idea. They are inexpensive, easy to install, and easy to use. Besides, some insurance companies will give buyers a discount on their home insurance if there's an extinguisher on the property.

Fire Sprinklers

Fire sprinklers are now required in almost all hotels and motels and in many commercial buildings. At some time in the future, they may be required in homes. As of this writing, I am not aware of any state in the country that requires them. Be sure to check with a good real estate agent in your area about current requirements, however. Fire sprinklers are invaluable in putting out a fire. There are often deep discounts on fire insurance policies available to homeowners or buyers who can demonstrate such a system exists.

If you're selling, unless such a system already is in place in the home, don't go out of your way to put one in. Particularly when retro-fitting, the expense can be enormous, sometimes several thousand dollars. On the other hand, if you're buying, safety concerns, an insurance premium discount, and your own peace of mind may make it worth the expense, especially if you plan on living in the house for a long period of time.

Is There a Water Hazard?

Water hazards in the home may be from polluted water or flooding. In some cases, you as the seller must have certain safeguards in place. In other cases, as the buyer you need to check certain areas with extra care to be sure there are no hazards, even ones the seller may not know of.

Every home contains at least two separate water systems: water suitable for drinking, and sewage water carried away from the home. As long as these two systems never come in contact with each other, chances are there will be no contamination problems in the home. However, if they do come in contact, anyone drinking the water could get seriously ill or die.

Well Water

If the property has a well, it is important that the well water be regularly tested, not only for toxic chemicals and metals but also for contamination. The most common contamination occurs when septic tanks are placed too close to wells, and sewage contaminates the drinking water. Sellers with wells on their property will want to present buyers with recent test reports. Virtually all buyers will want to examine these closely.

Septic Tanks

Septic tanks are really two systems: the septic tank itself, which separates the "gray water" or liquid sewage from the solid waste, and the leach field where the gray water dissipates into the soil. A leach field is typically a large plot of ground under which pipes have been placed, buried several feet deep, with small holes in them to allow the gray water to flow out into the soil.

To be sanitary, septic tanks must be periodically pumped to remove the solid waste. If they are not pumped, solid waste will rise until it flows out into the leach field, usually plugging it and making it inoperative.

A septic tank with a blocked leach field is considered a sanitary hazard. It could imperil the health and life of occupants of the property. If a blocked leach field is discovered by the county or city sanitation engineer, an order could be issued preventing occupancy of the property. As a buyer, you might not be able to live on the property while the leach field is replaced. Usually, a new field must be dug and can cost $2,500 or more.

As a seller with a septic tank, it's often a good idea to have the tank pumped and get a report on the operation of the system prior to selling the property. If there is no fee for dumping the sewage material, the cost is usually only around $100. A waste dumping fee could be several hundred dollars more.

The last thing you want to do is to sell or buy a property with an inoperative septic system.

Water Antisiphon Valves

Most houses with lawns have sprinkler systems. If the system is underground, it means that the same water that flows through the potable water system to the faucets in the home also flows to the sprinkler heads in the ground outside.

This is a potential problem because sometimes sprinkler heads will be underwater after a period of watering or there could be a leak in the pipe. When the water is turned off, a temporary backflow often occurs, which means that for a few moments the water can reverse direction. If the ground outside happens to be contaminated (for example, with fertilizer), some of the water that's been in that fertilizer could, in theory, be sucked back into the potable water system and contaminate the drinking water.

The most famous case of this occurred at the turn of the century in Chicago when a renowned actress was taking a bath in a hotel. The spout for the water into the tub was below the walls of the bath, and the water had reached the edges of the tub. When she turned the water off, some of the tub water flowed back into the submerged spout and into the potable water system. Later, she turned on the faucet in the sink, drank contaminated water from the tap, and died. That's the reason all tub water spouts are well above the top level of tubs today.

Something similar could happen with sprinkler and other outdoor water systems. That's why all such systems should have properly installed antisiphon valves. Typically, these must be several feet above the highest sprinkler head. They prevent water from flowing backward and potentially contaminating the potable water system.

Sometimes, those who install sprinkler systems simply aren't aware of this problem and don't properly install antisiphon valves. This is particularly true of older homes. Therefore, both as seller and buyer, you want to be sure that valves are there and are operating correctly. They are not expensive (about $20 apiece or less), and most gardeners or plumbers can do the job.

Be sure a city/county building department permit is obtained and that the installation is inspected.

Pressure Relief Valve

All houses have a hot water heater of some sort or another. Typically, these heaters use gas or electricity to generate heat. As the water temperature goes up, so too does the pressure in the tank. If that water temperature were to continue to go up in an uncontrolled fashion, it would eventually reach the boiling point and the water inside would turn to steam. When that happens, a catastrophe is in the making. When you turn on the hot water, scalding steam could come out. Or worse, the water heater could actually explode. (I've seen an entire house demolished from a water heater explosion.)

Although all water heaters sold today have safety systems designed to shut off the fuel that heats the water when the temperature gets too hot, these devices are not infallible. If these fail, the last safety device is the pressure/temperature safety relief valve. This valve is supposed to be installed on all water heaters. At a preset temperature and/or pressure, the value automatically opens and allows the water or steam inside the tank to vent safely to the outside.

Three potential problems can occur:

1. There is no safety relief valve on the water heater. Typically, this occurs when a previous homeowner installed the tank, was unaware of the need for this device, and didn't install it. (The

valve usually does not come with the water heater but must be purchased and installed separately.)

2. There is a safety relief valve, but it is old, corroded, or otherwise damaged and inoperable. This is no better than not having a valve at all.
3. There is an operable valve, but water from it is not vented safely outside. Instead, when activated it can spray around the heater and may scald someone who happens to be nearby.

As a seller, I feel you should make sure there is an operable valve that is properly vented. To do otherwise, in my opinion, opens the seller up to enormous and unnecessary liability. (Installing such a valve typically only takes a few minutes, and most homeowners following the instructions that come with it can handle the job. A professional such as a plumber also can do the work for you.)

As a buyer, I always personally check to see that there is an operable pressure/temperature valve on the water heater. Any good home inspector will do the same.

Testing the valve is quite simple. It will have a handle on it. Moving the handle will release the valve, allowing hot water to flow out. (Be sure to check where the water is vented to and be careful not to stand where you might get scalded!) If the water flows out freely, presumably the valve is operative. Unfortunately, the downside to this is that with some old valves, the process of checking them actually causes them to leak and you may end up having to replace them. (Also, be sure the vent pipe leading from the valve to the outside is metal, not plastic, which could melt in the event of a house fire.)

Other Water Hazards

Be sure there are no other water hazards in the home that may be peculiar to the area. This may mean determining if the house is in a flood basin. Although nothing can be done about this, as a seller, disclosure of this information to buyers will alert them to the danger. As a buyer, being aware of the flood hazard will allow you to purchase appropriate flood insurance.

What about Earthquake Hazards?

A majority of the United States could technically be called earthquake country. While the West Coast shakes and rumbles on a regular basis, other areas of the country have less frequent, but occasionally more severe earthquakes. For example, one of the most violent earthquakes recorded in recent history occurred about 100 years ago near the Missouri and Mississippi rivers.

As a seller, check with a good real estate agent to determine if there are any specific earthquake disclosure requirements in your area. For example, in California sellers must disclose if the home is in a geologically or seismically active area. This becomes so specific, in some cases, as to require naming the actual fault or seismic hazard zone.

As a buyer, you will want to know about the earthquake hazard in order to be able to purchase earthquake insurance (when available). Also, in some fault or hazard zones there may be specific retrofitting required before a home can be considered safe. This is something you'll want to negotiate with the seller. Check with your state or local earthquake commission.

Water Heater Strapping

One of the biggest problems when an earthquake hits has to do with water heaters. These are typically upright and very heavy when filled with water. (A 40-gallon water heater can weigh over 500 pounds.) Normally the weight of the water heater is enough to keep it from moving. However, when the ground itself begins to shake, the water heater can begin swaying and may topple over.

When an operating water heater tips over, there are a number of immediate and potentially disastrous consequences. Besides the release of high pressure water from broken water pipes (which though messy often doesn't present a catastrophic problem because most heaters are located in garages or storage areas), there is also the danger of broken gas pipes or electrical connections.

When the electrical connection is broken, there can be sparks and possible fire. When a gas service connection is ruptured, leaking gas can result in fire or explosion. During earthquakes in California, a large percentage of homes were damaged more extensively from fire from broken gas lines than from the earthquake itself.

For this reason, when selling a home in California and in other areas, the seller must disclose to the buyers whether that the water heater is properly strapped. Although the seller may not be required to strap it himself or herself, to my mind, doing so relieves me of an unacceptable level of concern. Normally, the water heater is strapped to meet the standards of the Uniform Building Code; however, additional strapping may be required in your area.

As a buyer, I always check personally to see that the water heater is strapped and ask that my home inspector check it as well.

It is not necessary to hire someone to strap a water heater. Instructions for proper strapping are widely available from state earthquake agencies. The materials required usually cost less than $20, and only simple tools are needed.

Earthquake Retrofitting

While strapping the water heater may be the most immediate problem, there are many other ground movement concerns in earthquake country. The following is a list of potential hazards found primarily in homes more than 40 years old.

As either seller or buyer, it's important to note that correcting the items in this list can involve very expensive retrofitting. I know of no state that currently requires earthquake retrofitting, though that could change in the future. My suggestion here is that sellers disclose any earthquake hazards and then consider doing the retrofitting work as strictly optional. For buyers in most areas, the same applies. Retrofitting can become a deal point, in which case buyer and seller must negotiate the costs or lose the deal.

Foundation anchors. In the past, particularly before 1940, some contractors simply built a foundation, put a mud sill (wooden bottom board) on top of it, and then built the home. They did not bolt the house itself to the foundation. In an earthquake, this means that the house can literally be shaken off its foundation. Besides causing severe damage, it also can result in the rupturing of water and gas pipes and the breaking of electrical wiring.

Retrofitting means going back and installing anchor bolts through the mud sill and into the foundation. If the foundation is solid cement, this is usually simple and effective. However, if the foundation is of some other material (such as rock or brick) or it is crumbling, retrofitting could require lifting the house and putting in a new anchored foundation—an extremely expensive task!

Cripple walls. A short wall (often two feet or less) is sometimes put on top of a foundation to create a crawl space under a house. These are called cripple walls. Because they are short, when the house sways because of an earthquake, these walls can collapse and, as a result, the house will fall, causing extensive damage as well as the chance for fire from broken gas lines or electrical connections.

Retrofitting usually is fairly simple. It normally just means going under the house and nailing plywood to the cripple walls. When properly nailed (sometimes the nails must be placed just a few inches apart on each stud), the cripple wall gains great structural strength.

Piers and posts. Similar to cripple walls, sometimes houses, particularly those on hillsides, will be built on posts that are supported by unconnected concrete piers. In an earthquake, the swaying motion can knock the posts off their piers and cause the house to collapse.

Retrofitting requires that either the posts be braced or, if that proves impractical, a new concrete foundation be poured beneath the affected portion of the house. This often requires the help of a good contractor and architect.

Unreinforced masonry foundations. We've already touched on this with regard to anchors. Unreinforced masonry foundations are typically stone or brick where a center area is filled with concrete. In modern construction, this center area also would contain reinforcing steel bars and anchor bolts. In older construction, these reinforcing elements are not present hence, in an earthquake, the foundation can crumble, causing the house to collapse.

Retrofitting here is usually quite expensive because it most often requires jacking up the house, removing the old unreinforced masonry foundation, and replacing it with reinforced concrete.

Unreinforced masonry walls. These are stone, brick, tile, adobe, or block wall surfacing that is simply built up, one piece at a time. In modern construction, these masonry walls are anchored by metal to the wall behind them. However, before 1940 these anchors typically were not present. In an earthquake, the wall front can collapse, possibly injuring or killing someone unsuspectingly standing beneath or nearby.

Retrofitting may require tearing down the existing wall and replacing it with reinforced masonry or other materials. Again, a very expensive job!

Unreinforced chimney.   An older chimney with no steel reinforcing can collapse, causing injury and severe damage in an earthquake. Often, bricks will come right through the ceiling or walls into the home.

Retrofitting usually requires replacing the chimney with reinforced masonry or other materials. An alternative, though not necessarily a good one, may be to install heavy plywood in the ceilings and wall near the chimney to prevent falling bricks from entering the home in the event of an earthquake.

Home over a garage.   This is a problem most homeowners aren't aware of; however, it can be serious. The large opening of a garage door provides a weak area in a structure. In an earthquake, the home may sway and the opening fail, causing the home above to collapse with severe damage.

This is usually easily retrofitted. A heavy piece of plywood is typically close-nailed on one or both sides of the garage door opening, provided there is sufficient room. This provides diagonal bracing to keep the area from shifting and collapsing.

What about Flood Hazards?

Flooding of property is usually, but not always, beyond our control. As noted earlier, when selling you should disclose any possible threat of flooding. As a buyer, you should investigate the possibility of flooding in the area, regardless of what the seller discloses. In other words, you need to make it your business to find out, even if there's only a remote possibility.

For example, the home might be in the flood plain of a river, but only if there is a 100-year or even a 500-year flood. Nevertheless, next year could be the one. As a seller, you need to disclose this. As a buyer, you must be aware of it.

The same holds true if the home is in the path of flooding if a dam should break. This is of particular concern in earthquake country.

Finally, those homes at the edge of coastal water could be subject to hurricanes or even tsunamis, large sea waves caused by an often distant earthquake. This is particularly the case for low-lying areas.

While there's little that can be done about such problems, disclosure lets sellers sleep easy and lets buyers at least have the chance of evacuation in the event they should be threatened.

Some potential flooding hazards can be corrected. These are caused by poor drainage, perhaps the number-one problem across the country when homes are bought and sold.

Typically, the problem occurs because the lot has not been properly graded. A well-graded lot will be higher in the rear and lower in the front, and the street will be lower than any portion of the property. This will result in water from rains flowing across the property and down the street. Too often, however, builders badly grade property so a portion in the rear or sides is low, causing flooding during rains. Often, this flooding results in water accumulating under the house.

Additionally, gutter spouts should be directed away from the foundation. Even if the property is properly graded, gutters draining water from the roof directly to the base of the foundation can cause flooding under the house and in basements.

Corrective measures often involve regrading the lot, something that can be very difficult to do when there is mature landscaping in place. Drain tiles, French drains, and even sump pumps also may be used. The cost for getting water away from the home and avoiding flooding from this cause can be as little as a few hundred dollars or as much as $10,000 or more. Failure to remove water from under the home can lead to foundation failure.

Generally speaking, as a seller you should disclose all possibility of flooding, bad drainage, and poor grading before the purchase is completed. As a buyer, you should pay special attention if the sellers disclose water problems, as well as investigate yourself to learn of any. If there are problems, you may want to back out of the deal (under your approval of a home inspection clause).

When drainage is an issue, as a buyer you can often demand concessions in price. As a seller, you can meet the demands or not.

What about Locks and Security Systems?

All homes have door locks. Some additionally have security systems. As a seller, you should inform the buyers if any of these are defective. (If there is a bad door lock, I always repair it prior to a sale.)

As a buyer, I always have the locks changed or rekeyed and the code on the security recoded before I move in. The reason here is that you can never be sure who has keys. When the seller turns over the keys to the property, presumably they have no other keys and will not attempt to reenter the home. However, as a buyer, how can I know if perhaps some work crew has a key? Or maybe a neighbor has a spare key? Or perhaps a relative or friend of the seller has a key? Changing or rekeying the locks avoids potential problems.

What If the Electrical and Gas Systems Aren't up to Code?

If the house is older, the electrical and gas systems may not be up to code. Indeed, they may not be safe by modern standards. This is particularly the case with homes that are more than 40 or 50 years old.

Disclosure of this fact is something sellers should do. In many cases, as a seller, I won't sell a property with a known problem but will have it fixed to protect myself. Buyers should be sure their home inspector checks out potential problems here.

Gas Problems

Unless there are leaking gas pipes, the biggest problems usually come from gas appliances that do not properly vent to the outside or that use inside air. Those that do not vent can cause occupants to become sick or, in the case of carbon monoxide poisoning, to die.

On the other hand, many newer houses are well insulated and extremely tight. In such cases, those gas appliances that use inside air for combustion can cause illness or even death by using up all the available oxygen in the house. The biggest problem here usually arises if the appliance is located in a small room, such as a bedroom.

Modern building codes normally prohibit the use of any gas or combustion appliance (such as a wood-burning stove) that does not vent to the outside. They also prohibit the use of gas or combustion appliances that use inside air in small areas such as bedrooms. (Some building codes outlaw them entirely.)

It goes without saying that as a seller you should disclose this information. However, I would not sell a home with a combustible appliance in it that was not up to the current building code and that could cause illness or death to occupants. The liability is simply too great. I would remove or replace the appliance.

As a buyer, once again, you should have your home inspector check for such appliances. Then, you can demand the seller replace them with appliances that are up to code.

There are a few other problems usually associated with combustible (typically gas) appliances. One of the most common has to do with gas (or other combustible) water heaters and dryers located in the garage. These use open flame to heat. However, a car parked in the garage whose fuel tank is not properly sealed (or has been overfilled) can leak fumes into the area. These fumes are typically heavier than air and move along the ground. When they come in contact with open flame (as from a gas water heater or clothes dryer), they could ignite, causing a horrendous explosion.

Therefore, most areas now require a combustion appliance located in the garage to be raised at least 18 inches off the floor. To my way of thinking, this is an absolute must. As a seller, it is not sufficient to simply inform the buyers of the possible hazards. The water heater and any other combustion appliance should be raised prior to the sale. As a buyer, if the seller refuses to do this, I wouldn't make it a deal point, but before moving into the property, I'd see that the appliance was raised (usually not a costly or difficult job).

Additionally, if a door leads directly from the garage into the house, car gas fumes can enter the home when the door is open. Besides being smelly, if a car is left running in the garage, carbon monoxide fumes could enter the home and cause illness or even death to the occupants.

Therefore, doors between the garage and the home should be sealed and should have a spring closing mechanism that prevents them from remaining open on their own. As a seller, this is not simply a matter of disclosure. Safety and your own liability demand that the door be properly sealed against fumes and a safety closing device be installed. As a buyer, check to be sure it has been done. If not, insist the seller do it. If the seller is foolish and refuses (and won't budge), be sure you have it done before you move in.

Electrical Problems

Generally speaking, there are relatively few electrical problems likely to exist in modern homes. However, these problems can be quite serious in older homes.

Broken, corroded, or deteriorating insulation on wires.
This can sometimes occur, particularly in homes built prior to 1950. When the insulation deteriorates, the wires can touch, causing sparking and fires. If the situation exists (it usually takes a home inspector who is willing to check the wiring in walls and ceilings to discover this), it's definitely a safety concern. Again, as a seller I don't believe disclosure is sufficient. Rather, I would have the bad wiring replaced. As a buyer, I would require the work be done before I move in. However, because this can be costly, you may want to make it a deal point.

Bad grounding.
Beyond bad wiring, most electrical problems have to do with improper grounding. To reduce the danger of shock, all wiring in homes that are up to modern building codes carry a ground wire. That means that three wires go to every outlet, normally white, black, and an uninsulated copper ground wire.

Some older homes, however, don't have that ground wire because years ago it was not required. Lack of the ground wire is something that definitely should be disclosed.

Further, lack of a ground wire where water is normally present, such as bathrooms and kitchens, could pose a serious safety hazard. I would recommend that all outlets in kitchens and baths have ground wires installed, if they do not exist.

Further, all receptacles in kitchens and baths should use ground fault interrupter (GFI) circuits. These are designed to quickly break the circuit if a person is receiving a shock. They only cost about $10 per receptacle, and often a half dozen or more can be linked to one unit. (They do, however, require a ground wire.)

Also, in most areas building codes require that the entire home electrical system be grounded to the cold water piping in the house, or a special electrical ground be sunk outside the home. This is usually not a problem, unless there has been some remodeling work done. Home remodelers sometimes come across the grounding wire connection to the plumbing, don't realize what it is, and remove it. Doing so creates an immediate hazard of shock from the home's entire electrical system.

As a seller, I want this work done to avoid potential liability down the road. As a buyer, I want my home inspector to look for and determine that the electrical grounding system is in place and operative.

Disclosure is not enough. The problem should be corrected before the sale is consummated, whether paid for by buyer or seller.

Aluminum wiring. Finally, some homes use aluminum wiring instead of copper. Aluminum is not as good a conductor, but by increasing the size of the wire, the same amount of current can flow through it.

Problems sometimes occur, however, when aluminum wiring is attached to receptacles, appliances, or even circuit breaker boxes, particularly if it is attached to copper. A special aluminum connector must be used in these cases, because over time the electricity flowing through the aluminum wire can actually cause it to unwind from where it is attached and cause a short.

Again, a good inspector is usually the one to identify such problems. If I were the seller, I would have the problem fixed. It is not costly. As a buyer, again if the seller refuses to have it fixed, I would be sure to have it done before moving in.

Index